THE 1895
SEGREGATION FIGHT
IN
South Carolina

THE 1895 SEGREGATION FIGHT
IN
South Carolina

DAMON L. FORDHAM

THE
History
PRESS

Published by The History Press
Charleston, SC
www.historypress.com

Front cover, top row: Robert Smalls and William J. Whipper of the 1895 South Carolina Constitutional Convention. *From the Library of Congress, public domain.* *Bottom*: The South Carolina State House in Columbia, South Carolina, 1890s. *From the Library of Congress, public domain.*

First published 2022

Manufactured in the United States

ISBN 9781467152761

Library of Congress Control Number: 2022935419

Notice: The information in this book is true and complete to the best of our knowledge. It is offered without guarantee on the part of the author or The History Press. The author and The History Press disclaim all liability in connection with the use of this book.

This book is dedicated to the memory of Abram Fordham Sr., Mary Fordham, James Buchanan Maxwell, Rebecca Mitchell Maxwell, Frank Montgomery, Minnie Carter Montgomery, Bristow Sheppard Sr. and Mary Sheppard. They are my ancestors who were alive in South Carolina in the late 1800s, and the main figures of this story fought to preserve their rights.

Call us aliens? We, aliens? The people who were the foundation of the American civilization, aliens? A people who, by their sweat, assisted in clothing the barren rocks of the Northeast in verdure, who drained the swamps of the South, and made them to mimic gold in harvest time; who, by their endurance, toil, and suffering, made it possible for our white neighbors to establish this government, the asylum of us all; who, by their toil, established the canal and railroad systems of this country—call us aliens? Then to whom can the term citizens be applied?

Thomas Ezekiel Miller
Black delegate to the 1895 Constitutional Convention
Columbia, South Carolina, October 25, 1895

CONTENTS

PREFACE

In 1998, I purchased a book called *Lift Every Voice, African American Oratory, 1787–1901* that was edited by Philip S. Foner and Robert James Branham (University of Alabama Press, 1998). Among the many forgotten addresses in this book was a speech by Thomas Ezekiel Miller, which the editors of that volume titled "A Plea Against the Disfranchisement of the Negro." This oration was Miller's protest against South Carolina senator Benjamin Ryan Tillman's efforts to deny the Black Americans of his state their right to vote under the Fifteenth Amendment and enforce segregation against them in schools. In 2018, the social commentator Ta-Nehisi Coates titled his volume of essays *We Were Eight Years in Power* (New York: One World, 2018) after a line in Miller's speech, and the title "Call Us Aliens" comes from a refrain from Miller's address.

It is widely known among those familiar with American history that by the 1890s, Black Americans had lost many of the rights they gained during the Reconstruction era, but few people today know about the resistance of Black people against these developments. I was so intrigued by Miller's eloquent arguments in his speech that I examined microfilms of the *Columbia State* newspaper and the *Charleston News and Courier* from the fall of 1895. These issues revealed that at the South Carolina Constitutional Convention of 1895, which Senator Benjamin R. Tillman organized to undo the Reconstruction era's social and political gains for that state's Black population, the six Black delegates made spirited efforts to thwart this convention's goals through presenting their case before the press of the world through their orations.

This event is scarcely known today, although three privately published pamphlets were made of their addresses. Maria Miller, the wife of Thomas E. Miller, published *The Suffrage; Speeches by Negroes in the Constitutional Convention: The Part Taken by Colored Orators in Their Fight for a Fair and Impartial Ballot* (Privately printed, 1896), but this volume includes only her husband's speeches and that of delegate James Wigg. Similarly, Sarah V. Smalls, the daughter of Civil War hero and delegate Robert Smalls, published *Speeches at the Constitutional Convention by Gen. Robert Smalls with the Right of Suffrage Passed by the Constitutional Convention* (Charleston, SC: Enquirer Print, 1896). A pamphlet of delegate Isaiah Reed's speech exists, but while these events were ably described in George Brown Tindal's *South Carolina Negroes, 1877–1900* (University of South Carolina Press, 1952) and Andrew Billingsley's *Yearning to Breathe Free: Robert Smalls of South Carolina and His Families* (University of South Carolina Press, 2007), and I have dedicated a chapter to these men's efforts in my own book *Voices of Black South Carolina: Legend and Legacy* (Charleston, SC: The History Press, 2009), of which this book is an extension, no complete collection of the speeches of these men has been compiled in any form until this present volume.

This book attempts to remedy that situation by gathering the known addresses of the Black delegates of the convention from contemporary newspaper accounts and from the couple who appeared in the "1895 Convention Journal." Curiously, the "1895 Convention Journal" did not record the full and complete speeches of the Black delegates, although a few appear. Additional material, including some historical background covering the Reconstruction era, some of the white delegates' remarks, educator Booker. T. Washington's open letter to Tillman regarding disfranchisement and some other historical material and primary sources, including those with an opposing historical view, have been added to provide further context to the story.

The modern reader should note that the documents from this period are presented as they were originally written, which means that much of the language used in regard to race would be offensive to sensitive readers today, so readers who have such concerns are advised to proceed with caution. The one concession I have made to current sensibilities is that the word *Negro* in reference to Black Americans was usually not capitalized at the time of these speeches and documents. I have chosen to capitalize the term in this book, as *Negro* was later understood to be a proper noun.

In reading the writings and speeches from Black South Carolinians defending their rights, it is interesting to consider that the arguments of these men and women would seem to be a matter of common sense to contemporary readers. It gives one pause to realize that some of the events of the twenty-first century have proven that public sentiment does not always align with what rational minds would consider as sensible, and in this aspect, the enclosed story may serve as a cautionary tale of what happens when public figures place political expediency over what they know to be correct.

Finally, at a time when inspiring and insightful oratory and clarity is rare, it is hoped that the publication of these speeches will inspire higher standards of public discourse for future generations, as well as solutions for the issues covered that remain in current generations. As Maria Miller stated in her introduction to the collection of her husband's speeches, "That the country may read these speeches and learn to know these brave and true men, I have edited a few of their arguments and prepared this pamphlet. I regard them as gems of Negro eloquence."

Damon Lamar Fordham
Mount Pleasant, South Carolina
2022

1

THE SETTING OF THE STAGE

The period after enslavement and the fall of the Confederacy was one of hope for Black Americans, particularly those in South Carolina. Charleston was liberated when a Black Union regiment, the Massachusetts Fifty-Fifth, entered the city that birthed the Confederacy and the Civil War in February 1865. While the white residents, who largely supported the Confederacy, mostly fled Charleston, Black Charlestonians celebrated in the streets, cheering the members of the Fifty-Fifth Massachusetts as liberators.[1]

Beginning in 1867, the "Radical Republicans" in the United States Congress embarked on a program to transform the defeated Southern states after the Civil War. Part of this transformation involved the changes in the status of Black Americans in these states. Defying (and later impeaching) President Andrew Johnson for opposing such reforms, congressmen such as Charles Sumner and Thaddeus Stevens called for the disfranchisement of some Confederates, the placement of federal troops in the Southern states and for the right to vote to be given to Black men and poor white Americans. As will be discussed further in this book, this led to a violent uprising on the part of many white Southerners. However, the freedmen quickly moved to take advantage of their new opportunities. From January to April 1868, seventy-six Black delegates (two-thirds of whom were formerly enslaved) and forty-eight white delegates met at the Charleston Club House on Meeting Street to compose a new constitution for South Carolina. Among the delegates was Robert Smalls, a formerly enslaved man from Beaufort, South Carolina, who, on January 23, 1868, proposed that South Carolina enact a public school system. Another Black delegate, William J. Whipper, would call for women to be allowed to vote, which did not pass. Delegate Alonzo Jacob Ransier, a Black Charlestonian of Haitian ancestry, became South Carolina's first Black lieutenant governor, serving from 1870 to 1872. He was succeeded by another Black South Carolinian, Richard Howell Gleaves, who served from 1872 to 1876.[2]

For years, books such as James K. Pike's *The Prostrate State*, Thomas Dixon's *The Clansman* and Woodrow Wilson's *History of the United States of America* have portrayed the Reconstruction leaders as being ignorant, incompetent and immoral. The following description of the Black South Carolina leaders appeared in Mary Simms Oliphant's *History of South Carolina*, which was used in various editions in the state's social studies classrooms until 1984.

> *More than half of the members of the legislature were Negroes, and most of these could neither read nor write. They spent nearly all of their time in the legislature in stealing the money of the people. Thousands and thousands of dollars were taken by these black thieves. Neither the property or the lives of white people were safe anywhere in the state....It must be realized that the state had a tremendous problem to face in the sudden liberation of irresponsible uneducated, unmoral, and brutish Africans.*[3]

The record shows that while a number of these men were indeed illiterate and dishonest, this was not the case of the whole. George D. Tindal noted this assessment in *South Carolina Negroes 1877–1901*: "Corruption in the government, it may be suggested, has been exaggerated to the neglect of important accomplishments. Chief among those were the establishment during those eight years of the principle of the equality of all men before the law and the right of all citizens to attend public schools supported by the state."[4]

The eligible voters of South Carolina went to the polls from April 14 to 16 in 1868 and voted to accept the new constitution, 70,758 votes to 27,228 votes. The 1868 Constitution tried to transform South Carolina into a democracy by forbidding cruel and unusual punishment and establishing public schools (regardless of race), divorce laws and antidiscrimination laws. The *New York Herald* noted, "Here in Charleston is being enacted the most incredible, hopeful, and yet unbelievable experiment in all the history of mankind." The Reconstruction Congress passed three constitutional amendments to secure these rights on a national level. The Thirteenth

Amendment in 1865 guaranteed that slavery would end throughout the United States. The Fourteenth Amendment, passed in 1868, guaranteed in article one:

> *All persons born or naturalized in the United States, and subject to the jurisdiction thereof, are citizens of the United States and of the State wherein they reside. No State shall make or enforce any law which shall abridge the privileges or immunities of citizens of the United States; nor shall any State deprive any person of life, liberty, or property, without due process of law; nor deny to any person within its jurisdiction the equal protection of the laws.*

The Fifteenth Amendment, passed in 1870, guaranteed:

> *The right of citizens of the United States to vote shall not be denied or abridged by the United States or by any State on account of race, color, or previous condition of servitude.*

However, Francis Cardozo, a delegate at the 1868 South Carolina Constitutional Convention, gave a prophetic warning before that convention.

> *It is a patent fact that, as colored men, we have been cheated out of our rights for two centuries, and now that we have the opportunity, I want to fix them in the Constitution in such a way that no lawyer, however cunning or astute, can possibly misinterpret the meaning. If we do not do so, we deserve to be, and will be, cheated again. Nearly all the white inhabitants of the state are ready at any moment to deprive us of these rights, and not a loophole should be left that would permit them to do it constitutionally. Not one of them scarcely was in favor of this convention, and just as soon as they had the power, whether by election of a Democratic president, or by an increase in emigration, they would endeavor to overthrow the Constitution. Hence, while they* [the Convention] *had a chance to do it, by all means, let them insert the words, "without distinction of race or color" wherever it was necessary to give force and clearness to their purpose.*[5]

Unfortunately, the promise of progress during Reconstruction was short-lived. Shortly after the dawn of Reconstruction, a meeting was held in Pulaski, Tennessee, on December 24, 1865. Six Confederate veterans, Captain John Lester, Major James Crowe, John Kennedy, Frank McCord, Calvin Jones and Richard Reed, formed an organization that would come serve as the violent army of resistance during Reconstruction. They named themselves after the Greek word for "circle," *kuklos,* and the Scotch-Irish word *clan,* for "family." This was the beginning of the Ku Klux Klan. The bloodshed of the Klan led Black Charleston congressman Robert Browne Elliot to testify before Congress about the Klan's brutality against Black residents and white sympathizers, leading President Ulysses S. Grant to pass the Ku Klux Klan Act of 1871, which outlawed the organization. Other violent groups, such as the Red Shirts and the Knights of the White Camelia, among others, continued to openly massacre Black Americans who attempted to vote and overthrow state governments. Eventually, in 1877, the Tilden Hayes Compromise withdrew federal troops who were sent to the South to protect the rights of Black Americans, and former Confederates regained their power. Black men were removed from public office in all but a few areas, and in spite of the Fifteenth Amendment's promise to allow Black men to vote, Black men were kept from the polls.

An example of this can be found in the following case. An 1878 South Carolina Congressional election featured a race between the Republican Edward A. Mackey and the Democrat Michael O'Connor. Mackey lost and sued on the grounds that O'Connor won through fraud, so O'Connor countered that Mackey induced illiterate Black men to vote. On November 12, 1879, the testimony in the Charleston County Courthouse revealed that many of the Black voters were in fact illiterate, but then James Buchanan "J.B." Maxwell of Christ Church Parish, South Carolina, was asked to testify. Maxwell was formerly enslaved, but unlike many of his immediate neighbors, he was a well-read graduate of Charleston's Avery Institute, and his answers took the counsel for the contested by surprise.

Deposition of J.B. Maxwell.
In the matter of the contest of E.W.M. Mackey against M. P. O'Connor.
STATE OF SOUTH CAROLINA,
Charleston County:

J.B. MAXWELL, a witness of legal age, produced by contestant upon due notice to contestee, deposes as follows in reference to questions produced by the contestant.
Question. How old are you?
Answer. Twenty-Four.
Q. Where do you live?

A. *Smithville, Christ Church Parish, four miles from Mount Pleasant.*
Q. *Where did you vote at the last election?*
A. *Mount Pleasant.*
Q. *What ticket did you vote?*
A. *The Republican ticket.*
Q. *Whose name was on your ticket for Congress?*
A. *E.W.M. Mackey.*
Q. *Did you vote more than one ticket?*
A. *No, sir.*
Q. *Were there any Democratic tissue tickets enclosed in your ticket?*
A. *Not one.*

Cross examination by G.R. WALKER, counsel for contestee:

Q. *How old are you?*
A. *Twenty-four.*
Q. *Can you read?*
A. *Yes, sir.*
Q. *You can?*
A. *Yes, sir.*
Q. *You read your ticket?*
A. *Yes, sir.*
Q. *You read all the names on it?*
A. *Yes, sir.*[6]

The condition of the Black vote deteriorated to the point that the following notice appeared in the August 29, 1892 edition of the *Charleston News and Courier*.

> *A separate list of all Negro voters must be kept and returned with the poll list. Every Negro applying to vote must produce a written statement by ten white men, who shall swear that they know of their own knowledge that such voters voted for [Governor Wade] Hampton in 1876 and have voted the Democratic ticket continuously ever since. This statement must be placed in the ballot box by the managers.*[7]

The intentional effect of this was to reduce the Black vote, but many Black Americans did not passively accept such subterfuge and soon organized against these efforts to curb their right to vote.

2

THE BLACK DELEGATES SPEAK

I n 1890, the State of Mississippi held a constitutional convention that was designed to strip its Black citizens of the right to vote in spite of the Fifteenth Amendment to the Constitution of the United States that was passed in 1870 to prevent such developments. Reactionary politicians in other states took heart from these developments and proceeded to follow suit.

Meanwhile, "Pitchfork" Ben Tillman (1847–1918), was elected governor in 1890. It should be noted that Tillman had a long history of open hatred toward Black Americans. In 1876, he was among the mob that massacred Black Americans in Hamburg, South Carolina. He rose to power in the 1880s, preaching a fair deal for the state's poor white farmers but also intense "Negrophobia." His openly professed goal was to strip South Carolina's Black population of political power. While his inaugural address in 1890 as governor of South Carolina promised Black residents relief from lynching, he turned over a Black man named John Peterson to a lynch mob in Denmark, South Carolina, in 1893.[8]

Amid such dire conditions, Bishop William D. Chappelle of the African Methodist Episcopal Church made this call to the *Columbia State* and *Charleston News and Courier* on September 21, 1893:

> *To the colored population, A Transmigration Association has been organized in Sumter, South Carolina, for the purpose of bettering the condition of our race. We mean to prepare to go to Africa or any place on the face of the globe. The condition of our people is alarming. Many are*

unable to feed and clothe themselves on account of the low wages which they receive for their work. In consequence of this fact, they have appealed to their preachers to look for them a more congenial field in which to labor for the necessities of life. For this cause, a meeting was called in, and the organization with the Reverend Isaac Miller as president and William D. Chappelle of Columbia as the corresponding secretary. All lovers of the race are called to meet in Sumter, on Monday, the 25th instant, to take further steps in this direction.[9]

The idea of migrating to Africa did not take hold among many. However, Black South Carolinians would organize again as Tillman was narrowly elected to the Senate in 1894. He felt that he nearly lost because of a divided white vote and united Black vote, the latter being against him. His solution was to disfranchise South Carolina's Black population without openly violating the Fifteenth Amendment to the United States Constitution, as was done in Mississippi by Governor James K. Vardaman in 1890. Thus, a constitutional convention was scheduled to be held at the South Carolina State House in Columbia to overhaul the progressive 1868 State Constitution, passed by seventy-six Black votes and forty-eight white votes in Charleston to guarantee equal rights for all citizens (excluding women's right to vote) and replace it with one calling for segregation and white supremacy.

Tillman laid his plans bare in an interview in April 1895. A Black reporter for the *Charleston Enquirer* met Tillman on a train in Augusta, Georgia, that was bound for Columbia. Surprisingly, Tillman offered the unnamed reporter his hand, offered the Black journalist a seat next to him and consented to an interview. When asked about his plans, Tillman replied, "One-half of these Negroes have no right to vote, they are too ignorant and venal. Besides, voting is no natural right. It is not a question of justice or injustice." He added, "We had a sample of what the Negro would do if he had power from 1868 to 1876, and that was enough. We don't want any more of it."

The Black journalist responded, "But the Negro gave you the best constitution you ever had. He gave the South your system of public schools."

Tillman avoided responding directly by saying, "Well, we propose to do everything the Constitution will allow us to do, and I don't see why these Negro ministers are kicking up such a fuss about it."[10]

The *Columbia State*, which was usually hostile to Tillman, printed a series of pseudo-Biblical lampoons of Tillman titled "The Chronicles of Zerrachaboam," which sharply satirized the senator. As early as 1892, one such entry stated, "Now in the fullness of time arose one Benjamin…who greatly deceived the people. The same was spoken by the prophet, saying, 'A one-eyed man shall be king among the blind.'" The *Columbia State* then wrote this witticism regarding Tillman's efforts to disfranchise Black voters: "He did wickedly seek by counting the ballots to change the great tablets of the law, so that the Sons of Ethiopia might no longer vote, and that he and his followers might reign forever."[11]

RALLYING AGAINST THE CONVENTION

On July 10, 1895, several months before the constitutional convention was to take place, about sixty of South Carolina's Black leaders convened in Columbia. Their purpose was to rally Black Americans and their white allies throughout the nation to use all peaceful, moral and legal means to stop the effort to disfranchise South Carolina's Black population. The following manifesto emerged as a result of this meeting, which appeared in the July 11, 1895 edition of the *Columbia State.*

An Appeal to Uncle Sam

To the people of the United States: as a part of the constituent elements from which our national government draws its life blood in time of peace and from whose life blood it exacts tribute in time of war, under broad reciprocal relations that should exist among all the people of one common country, that should be elastic, offensive or defensive weapons for every American citizen, however humble, at home or aboard, in order that the theory of government, handed down by the fathers might be fully realized and enjoyed by every individual on every inch of national territory, we submit that a small but desperate minority of the population has declared its purpose to perpetuate its power by unlawfully trampling under foot all the rights and franchises granted to us by the federal Constitution as a means of protecting life, liberty and property.

We have used every means in defense of our constitutional rights and franchise known to law-abiding citizens in this state without effect and as a last resort are forced to call the strong arm of the national government for a defense if rights granted and guaranteed by itself. As the army and navy are held as a reserve force to uphold local authorities in every state, the federal government, in order not to be imposed upon and used to support anarchy under the pretext of suppressing it, should see to it that a republican form of government, which we understand to be a government instituted by the sovereign will of a majority of the constitutionally qualified voters, actually exists in every state. We humbly crave your influence with the constituted authorities of the nation upheld so each American citizen might have equal protection of the law, without which constitutional guarantees are mere mockeries and life itself a mere burden to the people of the state.

We assure the fair-minded white people of the state that we are willing to use every means within our power to aid in the small but designing clique now in possession of the government, which has based itself in the reorganization of courts and militia for the purpose of perpetrating its power and which has been so emboldened with success in former revolutionary steps as to declare, under cover of the unconstitutional registration laws, its determination to hold a convention of its own make and liking and disfranchise the vast majority of the voting population regardless of constitutional prohibitions. It assigns as its reason for such unconstitutional and revolutionary steps that a constitution must be made to prevent what they are pleased to call Negro domination and to establish white supremacy. Which means, reduced to its essence, the supremacy of the faction now in control.

As the facts of history themselves prove, we deny that there has ever been a desire or attempt on our part to dominate the government. With the large body of us voting, most of whom are illiterate and poor, there is not as much danger of our control of the government as there is of the laboring classes in Massachusetts, New York or Pennsylvania, who, with unlimited suffrage contrasted with Tillmanite following, do not control. While we are entitled to participation in the government commensurate with our wealth and intelligence, representation is only a secondary consideration when compared with our right of suffrage, which cannot be annulled by any constitutional means.

Under our theory of self-government, in order that every man may possess the means within his person to protect life, liberty and possessions, the governing power is divided into as many fractional parts as there are male adults, to each of whom is deeded an equal portion designed to be used in a representative capacity and the ballot made its instrument.

As under our form of government, all officers and administrators of the law are designed to be creatures of the governed and are therefore the servants of all to whom they must look for return to or continuation in office, which means protection and happiness for all. The danger to the governed in such a form of government does not exist half so much in poverty or illiteracy as the accumulation of vast fortunes by the few, the influence of which may be used to swerve the servants of the people to administer the government or law in the interest of the few to the detriment of many.

Besides, if there is to be a privileged class government, restricted to persons possessing a certain amount of property or education, what reasons are there for not further restricting the governing class to a few college professors or millionaires? By making officers of the law, who should be the servants of us all, the dependent creatures of a class only, you make them, willing or unwilling, a tool of that class alone, and they would be bound to construe and administer the law to please members thereof only, by which system is apparent that the class born of power is without as much protection of slaves whose masters' ballots protect them. Such a form of government we had in a limited degree before the late war, when free Negroes, the underprivileged class, had to have guardians by whom many were deprived of their freedom and property.

Any form of government, if we may dignify it by such a term, which forces a class of people to contribute to existence without voice, whose contributions in the hands of the privileged class are used as engines of oppression, is worse than that among savages, where all men are at least equals.

By nature, God and the Constitution of the United States, we have been made freemen and guardians of our own rights, and our ballots given as peaceful weapons of defense, and no honest and loyal citizen is willing to deprive us of them, and we will fight the flesh, the devil and all his imps through every court and power in the nation before we shall be robbed of our rights by anarchistic nullifiers. A privileged government produces on the one hand, a class of cringing, suppliant cowards glad for the poor privileges of life for a short time, and on the other, a class of arrogant, cruel and heartless murderers, because conscious of wrongfully obtained power, whose members fear nothing from their creatures, the officers of the law, who construe and administer it as suits the will of their masters.

Such a government we have in the state today, and the ruling faction is in favor of handing it down in all its wickedness as a curse to generations unborn. But we are unwilling to entail such a legacy to future generations. Most of our murders and all our lynchings are immediately traceable to such a government, and under it, our state will continue to sink from bad to worse till it becomes such a hell [that] no one can live in it. Man, naturally given to error, is impelled to right action from only two causes—hope of reward or fear of punishment—and the law antedating the Mosaic age, that he that taketh a life must forfeit his own as a penalty, has been abrogated, and the rule in this state is that a white man taking the life of a colored man does not pay the penalty with his own, which has spread to others and is no longer confined to the oppressed class.

Upon the slightest provocation, members of the privileged class, without fear of punishment, murder or play [the] part of prowling savages or cannibals and dignify it by calling it a lynching, as the conscience of the state has been so seared that it is regarded as a virtue rather than a crime to lynch a fellow being. Murders and lynchings are noxious plants, flourishing only under a privileged class government, and will surely die when the sheriff and court are made dependent for future favors upon the suffrage of every man. We believe in universal suffrage, because we believe in the rights of all, which under our own form of government, cannot be secured without making a political power of each man equal in the creation of administrators under the law.

The most illiterate and humblest citizen, possessing nothing but his life and muscle, has as much right to the means of protecting his property, though invisible, as the millionaire. When deprived of our ballot, our influence with the administrators of the law is gone, and we are without protection. While all members of the privileged class do not take advantage of our helpless condition, many do, and it is cruel and hope-destroying to deprive us of the power to aid humane and liberal men in the election of such honest men as will in the dispensation of justice hold the scales equally balanced, whether the subject weighed is Black or white.

The rule adopted by the Democratic executive committee debarring all colored men regardless of past political affiliation from participation in the approaching primaries of said party and allowing all white men regardless of past political affiliation to participate in the same, with the declared purpose of counting in the general election the ones named in the primaries, is a violation of every principle of justice and honesty, repugnant to the doctrine of civilized government and a practical repudiation of the federal Constitution. We view with alarm the action of the conservatives, who are inclined to regard as broad and liberal, when they, to our exclusion and repudiation of our rights, accept and equal division with the administration faction and submit that it is most unreasonable to expect our support when failing to secure such concession.

We submit that the only honorable thing for them to do, if they mean justice, is to make a square fight for principle in every county in the state for the rights of all, in which they would get the support of every honest man in the state regardless of race or politics.

We further submit that we stand ready to join with any number of liberal white men of the state and aid them in making a constitution broad enough to cover the rights of every man, however rich or poor, and will only vote exclusively for delegates of our own race and party when such men fail or refuse to cooperate.

To the men of our race, we announce that no legal constitution can be made with our united opposition. We must organize to continue to raise means to prosecute the fight now pending in the federal court for the preservation of constitutional liberty to a final termination and to make such a showing in the approaching election as will enable us to move Congress to action through petitions. Before a final determination of the litigation, the proposed convention may beholden and all the wicked plans of our enemies incorporated into a new constitution, but if we shall prove it to the satisfaction of the Federal Supreme Court that in its making, all the rights and franchises granted us by the supreme Constitution have been ignored and trampled underfoot, of which we have no doubt, through fraudulent and unconstitutional registration laws, the new Constitution will amount to nothing, and our enemies will have their pains for the labor.

We congratulate all lovers of honest government in this state for the possession of at least one judge in the person of Chief Justice McIver, whose judicial ermine remains unsullied, and grieve to feel the time will soon come when our state will be deprived of the last of such tribunes.

Following the document, the *Columbia State* noted that the delegates then adopted the following resolution:

Resolved, that a state executive committee be appointed by the chair of this conference, consisting of one member from each county, to direct and manage the convention campaign for the state, each member of the state committee to be authorized to appoint one representative for each precinct to direct the campaign in his county.

Resolved, that we hold ourselves in readiness to join with liberal white men in every county who ask or may ask our support, but if none appear, we recommend that a ticket be nominated by our people and be voted on by them at the election for delegates to the constitutional convention.

Be it further resolved that the above method organization continue the work of organizing clubs and raising funds for the prosecution for honest elections now in progress in the federal courts and that this organization work in harmony with the ministerial union.

The *Columbia State* further stated:

Under the above resolution, the following were appointed.

Abbeville, Anthony P. Crawford
Aiken, S.E. Smith
Anderson, T.J. Harris
Barnwell, Thomas Clark
Beaufort, Samuel Green
Berkeley, P. Gilliard
Chester, Moses Binton
Chesterfield, H.L. Shrewsberry
Colleton, C.P. Chisolm
Charleston, W.J. Grant
Darlington, Dr. L.P. Daniel
Fairfield, Samuel Adams
Florence, S.W. Williams
Georgetown, Robert B. Anderson
Greenville, L.F. Goldsmith
Hampton, R.E. Primus
Horry, T.J. Gordon
Kershaw, A.W. Powell
Lexington, Jesse Miller
Laurens, P.S. Suber
Lancaster, F.R. McCoy
Marlboro, J.L. Cain
Marion, W.H. Collier
Newberry, D.T. McDaniels
Orangeburg, C.W. Caldwell
Richland, R.E. Hart
Sumter, R.H. Richardson
Union, W.D. Webor
Williamsburg, J.S. Thorp
York, T.F. Hunt
Spartanburg, H. Sims
Edgefield, J.A. Daniels
Clarendon, A. Collins[12]

Six Black delegates were eventually elected to attend the constitutional convention. Among them were Robert B. Anderson (listed previously) from Georgetown, Robert Smalls, Isaiah Reed, Thomas Miller, William J. Whipper and James E. Wigg, each from Beaufort County. Smalls and Whipper were among the Black delegates who drafted the 1868 Constitution, and on January 23, 1868, it was Smalls who drafted an amendment calling for the formation of public schools in South Carolina.

Another member of the executive committee mentioned previously deserves special attention. Anthony P. Crawford, the delegate from Abbeville, attracted national attention on October 21, 1916. A prosperous farmer in Abbeville, he was involved in a dispute when he accused a white store owner named W.D. Barksdale of cheating him over the price of cotton that Crawford harvested. The argument escalated, and Crawford was lynched in the town square by a mob ranging from two hundred to four hundred of the town's white citizens. Despite an extensive investigation by the National Association for the Advancement of Colored People (NAACP), no one was ever brought to trial and many of Crawford's relatives fled the area. During the summer of 2005, the United States House of Representatives and Senate apologized to the descendants of lynch victims, including Doria Dee Johnson, a great-great-granddaughter of Anthony Crawford. A short time later, on July 11, 2005, a worship service was held in Abbeville's Friendship Worship Center, where local white residents asked Crawford's grandson Eugene Crawford and other members of the Crawford family for forgiveness for the role of some of their ancestors in the lynching of Anthony Crawford. The Crawfords accepted the apology.[13]

THE BLACK CONSTITUTIONAL CONVENTION DELEGATES SPEAK

Six Black men who served in the delegation tried to stop Tillman during this convention. Two of these delegates, Thomas Miller and Robert Smalls, were major political rivals, but united for the cause of thwarting this convention. Five of the Black members sent the following letter to the *New York World* on September 30, 1895, shortly after the convention began. The "Mr. Creelman" in this letter refers to James Creelman, a correspondent to the *New York World* who wrote dispatches from this convention that were sympathetic to the Black delegates. The statements regarding the real reason for wishing to end Black voting in South Carolina are worthy of note.

Special to the World

COLUMBIA, S.C., SEPT. 30: Five of the six Negro delegates to the South Carolina Constitutional Convention, which proposes to disfranchise the Blacks, have joined in the following address to the North, through the World:

To the editor of the World.

The Seventh Constitutional Convention called in South Carolina is in session. It has been called for the purpose of dealing with the Negro problem. Those who have advocated its assembling have been explicit in their declaration of the purposes to be accomplished—the disfranchisement of the Negro and the elimination of him entirely, not from a participation in elections, for he has not since 1886 had any show at all in any of the elections held in the state, but the possibility of the Negro uniting with the conservative Democratic faction and thus oust from place and power those now in control of the government. The chief obstacle in the way of accomplishing what is desired is the Fourteenth and Fifteenth Amendments to the federal Constitution. This difficulty removed, there will be plain sailing.

The Honorable Benjamin Ryan Tillman, who is the head and front of the movement, has not been at all politic or hypocritical as to his intentions. He has said that his object is to disfranchise as many Negroes as he possibly can without disfranchising a single white man, except for a crime.

What the Census Shows.

In the state, according to the census of the United States, taken in 1890, there were: Negroes over twenty-one years of age, 132,949; whites over twenty-one years of age, 102,567; Negro majority, 30,292. Of these are illiterate, 58,086 Negroes and 13,242 whites. Now, it will plainly be seen that a purely educational qualification, honestly administered, would give the whites 89,415, and the Negroes 74,851 votes; white majority, 14,564 votes.

But the nut for Tillman to crack is how he can disfranchise the Negro without disfranchising the 13,242 illiterate whites, whose votes would be lost entirely to his faction should the conservative element nominate and vote an independent ticket. The highest vote his faction has ever been able to poll in around numbers is 60,000, and the conservatives 35,000. If Tillman's faction, therefore, should lose 13,242 votes, it would leave him only 46,758 votes, and the conservatives 35,000 votes, and Tillman's majority over the conservatives would be only 11, 758 votes.

It will readily be seen that the 74,851 Negro votes or any considerable part of them uniting with the conservatives would make that faction master of the situation, and that is what Tillman wants to prevent. He has thus far hypnotized the whites of both factions with the scarecrow "white supremacy," which he has shaken in their faces on every occasion and which he is shrewd enough to know has the same effect upon the whites as a red flag has upon an enraged bull.

Tillman's Suffrage Plan.

The real truth is that "white supremacy" has never been endangered; for even in the days of Republican ascendancy all the great offices, and a large majority of all the offices, were held by white men, no one ever thought of making it a Negro government. The suffrage plan, as we have been informed, as agreed upon by the committee, is as follows: every male citizen twenty-one years of age who has not been convicted of a crime and is not an idiot or an inmate of a prison or a charitable institution, who can read a section of the Constitution to the satisfaction of the officers of election, or who can explain said section when read to him to the satisfaction of said officers, or who pays taxes on $500 worth of real property; or who can satisfy the election officers that he has paid all his taxes due to him by the state, and who shall be duly registered according to law, shall be entitled to vote.

Every one of these provisions, as simple and just as they appear, when read by the uninitiated, are fraught with fraud, corruption and prostitution of the suffrage. For the officers of the election are the sole judges of the qualifications of the elector and can, at their will, make the Negro vote or the white vote as large or small as they choose.

Every one of those innocent little "ors" is the instrument of and contains infinite possibilities of fraud, and in the hands of election officers, all of whom are members of one party and of the same faction, are constructed to mean one thing to one set of votes and another thing to another set, when they offer to register.

As Mr. Creelman has explained in his dispatches, the registration officer and his board will have the sole power to make voters in South Carolina, as the Supreme Court of the state has decided there is no appeal to any court of law from the acts of election officers. In short, the convention has been called to legalize the frauds which have been perpetrated upon the elective franchise of this state since 1876. No one can tell or estimate *what the vote will be, and that question can be answered only by the election officials.*

Robert Smalls,
Thomas E. Miller,
James E. Wigg,
Robert B. Anderson,
Isaiah Reed
Republican Members of the Constitutional Convention. Columbia, SC, September 30, 1895.[14]

ISAIAH REED'S ATTEMPT TO CURB LYNCHING

Early in the convention, Isaiah Reed of Beaufort tried to curb lynching with the following proposal for the state constitution.

Mr. I.R. REED introduced the following resolution, which was read the first time and referred to the Committee on Declaration of Rights:

RESOLUTION FOR THE PROTECTION OF PERSONS CHARGED WITH CRIMES AND MISDEMEANORS.

Be it resolved and ordained by the people of the state of South Carolina, in convention assembled, and by the authority of the same, that the following provisions shall constitute Section — of Article — of the constitution of this state:

Section —. That the governor of this state is hereby empowered and required to suspend or remove from office any sheriff, deputy sheriff, jailor or constable who allows or suffers any person charged with a crime or misdemeanor to receive any personal injury from any source whatever, except by due course of law, while in the custody of any one or more of them.

Section —. That the governor of this state is hereby empowered and required to call out and send one or more companies of the militia of this state to the assistance of any sheriff, deputy sheriff, jailor or constable when the emergency demands or on information and belief that violence is

31

threatened against a prisoner or any one or more of the above-named officers having a prisoner in custody.

Section —. That the governor of this state is hereby empowered and required to appoint, forthwith, any person to take the place or office of such sheriff, deputy sheriff, jailor or constable suspended or removed as aforesaid, whose term of office shall be until such suspension is removed or removal restored, and whose fee or compensation shall be such as are regulated by the legislature of this state.[15]

This amendment was soundly defeated.

Robert Smalls on Interracial Marriages

During the 1800s and early 1900s, interracial relationships between the sexes was a major issue. In the era of slavery, white men had unlimited sexual access to Black women, especially those who were enslaved, but Black men were often killed for giving the slightest suggestion that they wished to be involved with white women. While marriage between the races was scorned, many white men of this era had Black concubines, all of which made interracial relationships a controversial issue for many years. However, it was not until the 1895 South Carolina Constitutional Convention that interracial marriage was to be outlawed in that state. Robert Smalls shocked the convention with the following statement on October 2, 1895. The "Mr. President" referred to here and in the other addresses was South Carolina governor John Gary Evans, who was the president of the convention and who had pledged to continue Tillman's policies.

The convention having under consideration the Legislative Department Ordinance, when Section 34 was reached, which reads:
"The marriage of white persons with a Negro or mulatto, or person having one-eighth or more of Negro blood, shall be unlawful and void"; he [Robert Smalls] *proposed an amendment adding after the word "void" in the second line, the words "and any white person who lives and cohabits with a Negro, mulatto, or person who shall have one-eighth or more of Negro blood, shall be disqualified from holding any office or emolument or trust in this state, and the offspring of such living or cohabiting shall bear*

the name of the father and shall be entitled to inherit and acquire property the same as if they were legitimate."

Mr. President: I hope this amendment will be adopted. Sir, there is not a colored man or woman of any respectability, not only in South Carolina, but in the whole country, that does not oppose the intermarriage of races. There are very few, if any, exceptions in South Carolina, where a white man ever married a respectable colored woman or a colored man ever married a respectable white woman. The facts in this case are that the white woman who marries a Negro man as a rule has been the outcast by her race, and the colored woman that marries a white man has no standing with the respectable women of her race, and the white man no better with his. I cannot see why you would want to prevent the intermarriage of the races, when they want to legitimize their actions, unless you adopt my amendment, prohibiting the cohabitation of white men with Negro women. Mr. President and gentlemen of this convention, let me give you a little statistic, showing you, if it is possible to do so, the wrongs you or your forefathers have done to my race. Let us stop it, if we can. I fear not, but let us put it in the fundamental laws of this state.

"The number of Americans of African descent, wholly and in part, returned to the census bureau in 1890 was 7,470,035. These were divided as follows: Pure Africans, 6,337,980; mulattoes 956,987; quadroons, 105,132; octoroons, 69,936. The total mixed bloods, white and Black, was 1,132,060 in the whole country, and a third of these are above the Mason and Dixon line."

Mr. President, a careful perusal of the census, also history, shows that more than three-fourths of the mothers of this large numbers of mixed blood whom you seek to legislate against, are colored women. If so, who could have been their fathers? Do not any of you rise and deny this, because I am no lawyer, but know enough that I cannot impeach my own witness. A careful perusal of the census also shows in this state that this one-fourth that lives beyond Mason and Dixon's line shows fully that three-fourths of the one-fourth of the mixed blood were born in the southern states. So you see, gentlemen, you are responsible for the wrongs that have been done. Let us in the name of God and in behalf of virtue try and put a stop to this cohabitation. I could but admire a few days ago, when the gentlemen upon this floor spoke so highly of the women of this state, I am mindful of the fact that when they spoke of the women of this state that they spoke of the white women. I can but echo their sentiment and do say that I believe them to be as pure women as can be found anywhere in the world. I have not been strongly in favor of female suffrage, but since your discussion on the divorce law, I feel I shall vote for the suffrage in order that they may pass a law or laws that will make you as pure as they are.

We have, sir, as pure colored women in South Carolina and in this country as any race upon this earth. Sir, that evil known as slavery caused all of this. This wrong was done by you all owning them as your slaves. Sir, no act of yours will prevent a white man from marrying a colored woman or a colored man form marrying a white woman, who have the means to go in another state. There are many states in the Union that do not prevent them from marrying, and they can go and get married, and you cannot help yourself. I have in my mind distinctly a colored man and a white woman who were in love with each other and who wanted to get married, but this man recited to her the law on your statute book that prohibited the intermarriage of the races. This lady stated that there were no such laws in the District of Columbia, New York or Massachusetts. She was as pure a lady as there is. I only cite this because it is a matter that you cannot control except directly in the state.

This entire matter, sir, has no right in the constitution of the state. If your women are as pure as you stated, and I have reason to believe that they are they can be trusted, then why the necessity of having this placed in the constitution? Can you not trust yourselves? Is it because that these wrongs have been perpetrated here, since the formation of the government, that you feel that you can't be trusted? When I say you, I mean the white men of the entire state. I fear not, hence I trust the amendment will be adopted. These wrongs have been done and are still being done. It is not done by colored men; it is done by white men. If a Negro should improperly approach a white woman, his body would be hanging on the nearest tree, filled with air holes before daylight the next morning—and perhaps properly so. If the same rule were applied on the other side, and white men who insulted or debauched Negro women were treated likewise, this convention would have to be adjourned or die for lack of a quorum.

The gentleman called me to order, stating that I had reflected on the convention. I do not wish to reflect on the convention but do say that if he has clean hands, he will keep his seat, because I do not mean to reflect on any man who objects to the intermarriage of a Negro or Mulatto woman with a white man and is willing to prohibit the cohabitation, which is the root and the branch of this evil. Stop this evil, and there will be no occasion for this intermarriage law. Sir, I oppose the intermarriage of the races as strongly as you do, and I feel that I echo the sentiment of the respectable class of both sides; because with few exceptions, we find these marriages are among the lower element of both races, and therefore, they degrade and not elevate either race.

But sir, don't tell me that you will make a law to prevent lawful marriages and give full license to illicit marriages. Watch the census of each decade, and you will clearly see that this vice is decreasing among our people; as they are progressing educationally, they are raising themselves out of this degradation that your race has placed upon them. Now sir, I say prohibit intermarriage of the races, also make a law as binding against cohabitation. Then you will make your men as true as your women. And our race will be freed from a vice that is as degrading as the system of slavery. Again sir, on behalf of my race, I hope that the amendment to the section under consideration will be adopted and become a part of the constitution of the state.[16]

In a pamphlet that collected her father's speeches at this convention, Sarah Voorhees Smalls stated, "The introduction of this amendment caused a great deal of discussion, which showed plainly that South Carolina had no idea of punishing white men for wrong done to colored women, nor would she allow the wrong to be rectified, and the original Section 34 was adopted and is now the fundamental law of the state." However, on October 17, 1895, page 5 of the *Charleston News and Courier* printed an outlandish headline titled "All Niggers, More or Less!" This article quoted the convention's president, George Tillman, making the following remarks about the legalities of interracial marriage in South Carolina.

If the law is made as it now stands, respectable families in Aiken, Barnwell, Colleton and Orangeburg will be denied the right to intermarry among people with whom they are now associated and identified. At least one hundred families would be affected to my knowledge. They have sent good soldiers to the Confederate army and are now landowners and taxpayers. Those men served creditably, and it would be unjust and disgraceful to embarrass them in this way. It is a scientific fact that there is not one full-blooded Caucasian on the floor of this convention. Every member has in him a certain mixture of Mongolian, Arab, Indian or other colored blood. The pure-blooded white has needed and received a certain infusion of darker blood to give him readiness and purpose. It would be a cruel injustice and the source of endless litigation, of scandal, horror, feud and bloodshed to undertake to annul or forbid marriage for a remote, perhaps obsolete, trace of Negro blood. The doors would be open to scandal, malice and greed; to statements on the witness stand that the father or grandfather or grandmother had said that A or B had Negro blood in their veins. Any man who is half a man would be ready to blow up half the world with dynamite to prevent or avenge attacks upon the honor of his mother in the legitimacy or purity of the blood of his father.[17]

Robert Smalls took the floor again and responded as follows.

The Negro question has called the convention, but this section and this debate admits to the world that you have a people tainted with Negro blood. Let us make a constitution of which everyone may be proud. There is no need for the section. You have said to the world that the worst part should not stand, and the best part should be killed of the resolution that I had the pleasure of introducing. The evil is the cohabitation, not the marrying. We are not going to outstrip you. We are going to stand by the virtue of the women of our state. If the colored race was in any trouble in this respect, the white people were responsible for it. No people who have drunk from the cup of liberty would ever again be slaves.[18]

The delegates agreed to let what would become Section 34 remain adopted as written. On June 12, 1967, the United States Supreme Court ruled in *Loving v. Virginia* that state bans on interracial marriage were unconstitutional. This included the ban in South Carolina, but the ban remained in the state constitution. Finally, on November 3, 1998, exactly 103 years, 1 month and 1 day after Robert Smalls's speech, South Carolina voters voted to remove Section 34, which banned interracial marriages, from its state constitution with a majority of 62 percent of votes cast in favor of its removal. This was covered in the *Columbia State* on November 4, 1998.[19]

CALL US ALIENS?
THOMAS MILLER SPEAKS ON VOTING RIGHTS

On October 25, 1895, Thomas Miller (1849–1938), a Black man of mixed racial ancestry, rose to speak in favor of the voting rights of South Carolina's Black population during the constitutional convention that was designed to curb these rights. Miller was born free in Ferebeeville, South Carolina, and grew up in Charleston. After attending the University of South Carolina during Reconstruction, Miller served as a school commissioner and congressman from Beaufort Country, South Carolina. The October 26, 1895 edition of the *Columbia State* that is the source of this document mockingly referred to Miller as "Canary Miller" due to his light complexion. Miller made the following lucid and potent speech in response to Tillman and his followers. Despite its length, this speech's content, eloquence and historical importance make it necessary to reprint the message in its entirety for the first time since 1895.

The *Columbia State* of October 26, 1895, reported that the previous day's session was to deal largely with the issue of Black voting. Benjamin Tillman was given twenty-five minutes to make an introductory speech, in which the printed remarks show his repeated use of the epithet "nigger." James Wigg, one of the Black delegates, asked Tillman if he approved of a bill to place a tax on emigration from South Carolina. Tillman replied, "I would be glad to see every Negro leave if he wanted to."

It was in this atmosphere that Miller made the following address.

> *Mr. President: As an American citizen, as one who yields to no man in respect for the laws of the United States and South Carolina, as one who loves the past history of our nation and the dear old state when that history has been for the good and benefit of mankind, as one who never by word or vote committed an act that in any way tended to destroy the rights of any citizen, white or black, as one who wishes to see every male citizen— and woman, too—who is not disqualified on account of crime or mental condition the equal of any other citizen in the enjoyment of inalienable rights, the chief of which is to have a voice in the government, I approach the discussion of the proposed disfranchisement of the common people of South Carolina, white and Black.*
>
> *Mr. President, the conservative force in our state is the common people, the burden-bearing people, and sir, when you say that $300 and the capacity to read and write are the requirements to be possessed by voters, you are striking at the root of the tree of universal government. I ask in the name of the brotherhood of man and equal citizenship of the American people that I should not be trammeled by rules making my stay a short one. I ask the forbearance and the necessary time to discuss this all-important question, and I do hope and believe that, although I am in a feeble minority, this all-powerful majority will hear me, because I approach the discussion with*

malice toward none, but with a loving hope that the final settlement of this very vexed question. May the spirits of departed patriots, who have shed their blood for the rights of man on this soil bear witness of our condition and in some way hover over us and guide us to the right.

This fight against the right of the common people is not a new one. More than two thousand years ago, Julius Caesar, as the head of his solid phalanx, shattered the Roman empire and established a government and secured to the people the right to raise their voice in their own behalf. But in time, the lords of the empire gained control and the voice of the last tribune was hushed in that government. Later, under the feudal lords in Europe, the white peasants were nothing more than white slaves. They were so insignificant in the eyes of the barons that in France, every peasant was known as "Jack," and there was on the "Jacks," as it is called in history, is a blot on the page of Anglo-Saxon civilization that harrows up the soul of a freeman, and when he reads it, he becomes overwhelmed with grief and indignation that his forefathers could have so brutalized and degraded their white fellowman.

In this fight, the feudal lords overthrew the peasants, and their lot became harder and harder. Later, right across the English Channel, the white slaves of Britain were so thoroughly outraged that one great commoner and leader of the people for equal rights under the government, Oliver Cromwell, caused the English throne to totter and drove therefrom the insolent and inhumane Charles I. But finally, wealth and avarice, greed and intolerance united, and the common people went down. The French Revolution was caused because a white peasant was forbidden to kindle a fire upon his hearth in which to parch his corn and roast his black bread. The feudal lords compelled them to send their corn and dough to the public ovens to be baked so that a heavy toll could be taken therefrom. If a peasant in his holdings made $640 in one year, the lords and the church took from him the $600 and left him and his family but the $40.

Hand in hand with a united effort, the white man and the Black reclaimed this country and made it the asylum of the oppressed from every climate. And here today, Mr. President, after a residence of more than 250 years, with love and affection for the government, after having borne our part in every struggle and answered to every call, after having proven to the world that we are conservative in thought and action, loveable in our natures, forbearing toward our oppressor, living under and by the laws at all times, we are confronted at this hour, the noonday of peace and unity in this nation, the noonday of prosperity and hope, the noonday of this magnificent existence of ours with this proposition to disfranchise the common people; to take from them the dearest right, the right to vote.

Oh, Mr. President, why is this to be done? Is there anybody here who can or dare deny that the sole purpose for which this convention was called for is the disfranchisement of the common people, and the Negro more especially? If there is such a person, I ask him to read the speeches of the leaders who forced this convention upon us against the will of the people, and they will all be convinced that the only thing for which this convention was called is for the disfranchisement of that class of people, whose chief lot it has been to toil, toil, toil. With no hopes but to toil! Then if the speeches leave any reasonable doubt, I ask him to read this article by Senator Irby as a political monstrosity, and he will be thoroughly convinced that the purpose for which this convention was called is to disfranchise the Negro in the rice fields and his poor, uneducated white brother, who plows the bobtail ox or mule in the sand hills.

He will be convinced that this convention was called to disfranchise the Negro in every walk of life and the poor white boy who edits a newspaper in which he speaks fulsomely for the greatest of all misnomers and southern bugbears—white supremacy. There is no hope for him, though he wields an eloquent pen, if he is poor. His forefathers may have come here, and, like the Negro, spilt his blood, shed his tear and toiled to plant this magnificent tree of liberty, but if this monstrosity becomes law, there is no hope for him but to toil and grovel in poverty, because for the want of $300, though an educated Caucasian, he is no better off than his ignorant brother in Black skin.

Trickery is not legislation. These little innocent "ifs" and "ors" may in the hands of skilled manipulators or fraudulent registration entice the poor, illiterate white men to vote at one or two succeeding elections, but in less than six years, under the part of this law, saying that a man who cannot read and write a section of the constitution, that a man cannot vote who does not own $300 worth of property, a governor will be elected who will turn the machinery over to the wealthy, to the managers of corporate rights, to the gold bugs, to the whiskey trust, and we will have a spectacle like this: the poor, ignorant white man; the poor, educated white man; the poor, ignorant Negro; and the poor, educated Negro will be nonentities in the government, with no voice to say who shall rule, with no representation in the legislative halls, with no representation in the courts; it will be turning back the wheel of progress, and revolutions should never go backward.

Mr. President, it has been said that the purpose of this article of franchise is to disfranchise the Negroes, and I read you the exact of that slogan of *reform, the Honorable Benjamin R. Tillman. He makes it clear for what purpose he called this convention.*

From the *Times and Democrat* of Orangeburg, South Carolina.

The Suffrage Question: How Senator B.R. Tillman Proposes to Fix It.

Branchville, July 24: When I wrote the summary of the suffrage schemes discussed with the leaders, which I send in with this, I had no idea that it was so soon to receive direct corroboration from the man who has been the head of the Reform movement from its very inception. But at a meeting held at Hunter's Ferry, ten miles from this place, in Barnwell County, Tuesday, Senator Tillman made a speech in which he handled the matter, and I am able to quote the exact language on the scheme. He said:

"Any scheme that may be adopted can only be temporary, and it will be largely dependent upon white unity, as it lies in the administration of the law rather than in its language we must rely. This has been the case with the registration law and the eight-box law. As long as no discriminating on account of race or color can be made, even an educational qualification, pure and simple, would only serve its purpose of disfranchising the Negro while he remains ignorant. How then can we disfranchise illiterate Negroes without at the same time taking the right of suffrage from that class of white men? It is easy enough and cannot be called a fraudulent system. The Mississippi Constitution provides that every voter must be registered, and that the applicant must be able to read a clause in the Constitution or be able to understand it when read to him. The right to judge the latter rests with the supervisor of registration. If the applicant can read, he must be registered and allowed to vote.

If he cannot, it is easy to see that the Negro could not understand, while the white man would. Now you can see how many thousands of Negroes will be disfranchised without fraud or without infringing on the Fifteenth Amendment to the United States Constitution. Should we ever have a government that would appoint registration officers who wanted the Negroes as voters, this scheme would not work. But there is a difference between having it in the Constitution and depending on the eight-box and registration laws. A defeated minority of white men could never obtain control of the government by using the Negro vote. Such a minority must obtain control of the government by obtaining a white majority first, and it would then have no need for the Negro."

The senator says here that it is in the manipulation of the law and not in the words by which they expect to see the Negro disfranchised. He says plainly that the Negro will not understand the section when read to him because he is a Negro and the man who will judge of his understanding will be a white man. Is that denied? I will pause for a denial or any explanation of the language quoted.

Why do they say the Negro must be disfranchised? Is it because he is lawless? No! Is it because he is riotous in the discharge of the right of suffrage? No! They answer, "Because his skin is Black, he should not vote. Because his skin is Black, he is an inferior. Because he did not fight for the ballot, he should not have it. Because we are a conquered people and were conquered by the national government, in the name of the Negro, he shall not vote."

Mr. President, these are some of the reasons given by those who swear by the altar of liberty that we shall not be citizens. Why have they thus sworn? Mr. President, this country and its institutions are as much the common birthright and heritage of the American Negro as it is the possession of you and yours. We have fought in every Indian war, in every foreign war, in every domestic struggle by the side of the white soldiers from Boston Common and Lake Erie to the Mississippi Valley and the banks of the Rio Grande.

The first universal struggle was the Revolutionary War against British oppression, and the first drop of blood that was spilt in that struggle was shed on Boston commons by a Negro slave, Crispus Attucks. In that conflict, he and three white Patriots gave up their lives for this priceless liberty that we now enjoy, and the masters of the Black slaves and other free white men united to do this fallen hero homage, and as a token of their high respect and valor, they buried him and his three white comrades in a single grave. The day when the white men of Massachusetts buried those white heroes in one and the same, a united and common grave with this patriotic Negro, the status of the Negro in America was irrevocably fixed. Sirs, for seventy-five years after that conflict, the wheel of progress toward the universal rights of all was stopped and the cause of the Negro was hopeless. But—

"Justice, like a volcanic fire,
May sleep suppressed awhile,
But can't expire."[20]

The convention took a recess until 7:30 p.m., and the *Columbia State* of October 26, 1895, reported that as Miller resumed, "The galleries were jammed, among the audience being many young ladies from Columbia's female colleges." Miller continued with a discussion of the role of Black people in the American Revolution:

> *In that struggle, more than eight thousand Negro slaves and freemen were regularly mustered into the colonial army. They fought in every battle, and no historian records that they ever deserted the flag of freedom or allowed it to trail in the dust.*
>
> *South Carolina furnished the beggarly number of 6,417 white soldiers. Think of it! We read that this great colony, after having produced the greatest amount of brain and the strongest of those in the Revolutionary struggle was so overrun by Tories that she only furnished 6,417 during the entire war.*
>
> *I need not remind you that at the Battle of Camden, white Carolinians threw down their arms, disobeyed orders, and became mutinous in the very presence of invading foes. Here, I read to you what General Thomas [Sumter] said in his letter to John Adams about the worth of the soldiers that were in his ranks:*
>
> *"At Roxbury, we have some Negroes in our army, but I look on them in general as being equally serviceable with other men for fatigue, and in action, many of them have proven themselves brave. I would avoid all reflection or anything that would tend to give umbrage, but there is in this army from the southward [states] a number called riflemen who are the most indifferent men I have ever served with. These privates are mutinous and often desert to the enemy, unwilling for duty of any kind; exceedingly vicious, and the army here would be as well off without them. But to do justice to their officers, they are, some of them, likely men."*
>
> *I do not make this history that I have read. It is the white man's history. I read what he says about Negro soldiers with pride and love and what he says about the soldiers from the southward with tears of sadness, with tears of regret and account for their conduct under the one colossal excuse that being mostly of the master class, they were like spoiled children and could not yield to the rod of discipline and order.*
>
> *When all hopes had been crushed in South Carolina and Tarleton and the invading foe had run over the country and destroyed the sweets of domestic happiness here and the colony of Georgia had laid waste, our own Henry Laurens wrote General [George] Washington, saying: "If you permit me to arm three thousand Negroes of my native state, I will place myself at their head, and drive every Briton and Tory from the soil of freedom in South Carolina, Georgia and Florida."*

But all the arms that the struggling colonies had then were in the hands of enlisted soldiers, and Henry Laurens, on account of the impoverished condition of the colony, was never permitted to arm his faithful, patriotic 3,000 Negroes. Maryland alone enlisted into the colonial service more than 750 Negroes who fought and died in the cause for liberty for all.

The number furnished by old Virginia was so great that it was necessary for the legislature of that commonwealth, when peace was restored, to pass an act emancipating all slave Negroes who had enlisted in the Continental army and had fought the battle of the common people until liberty to all was inscribed upon the escutcheon of this nation.

And sirs, I beg to read to you what the prince of orators, one of South Carolina's brightest jewels, Charles Pinckney, said about the Negro upon the floor of congress during the Revolutionary struggle. He said:

"It is a remarkable fact that notwithstanding in the course of the revolution in the southern states were continually overrun by the British, and that every Negro in them had an opportunity of leaving their owners, but few did, proving thereby not only a remarkable attachment to their owners but the mildness of the treatment from whence their affection sprang. They were, as they still are, as valuable a part of our population to the Union as any other equal number of inhabitants. They were in numerous instances the pioneers and in all the laborers of your army. To their hands were owing the erection of the greatest parts of the fortifications raised for the protection of our country, some of which, particularly Fort Moultrie, gave at the early period of the inexperienced and untried valor of our citizens' immortality to American arms; and in the northern states, numerous bodies of them were enrolled and fought by the side of the whites in the battles of the Revolution."

The confidential spy and bodyguard of Lafayette was a Virginian Negro slave [author's note: his name was James Armistead], *and I have heard Alexander H. Stephens* [vice-president of the Confederacy] *say that by Virginians, there was no Revolutionary Patriot held in higher esteem than the Negro slave, Lafayette's faithful spy and bodyguard.*

The valor of the Negro in the War of 1812 is known in part. Negro seamen defended our commerce upon the high seas in every naval combat, and Peary's great victory on Lake Erie was fought to the finish by the assistance of large numbers of Black seamen. And the historian recording the valor of those faithful Black tars said that the cause of liberty could never suffer as long as the colonies produced such faithful, patriotic and heroic Black sons. In that war, the State of New York also furnished two regiments of two thousand Negro soldiers who met death upon the field of battle in the cause of this priceless privilege that you are about to take from us. At the Battle of New Orleans, [Andrew] Jackson's right, where he stood himself, was covered by two Black battalions that constituted part of his army. In singing the praise of those who have fallen in the cause of freedom and universal rights, not one word is applicable to the white Patriot that is not absolutely true when they are applied to the Negro soldiers in all of our struggles.

But Mr. President, although we have purchased this land of our birth by our past deeds, you and yours say that we must not vote, because we are an alien race. Aliens, say you, because our skins our Black. But oh! Mr. President,

'Tis neither birth, race clime or claim
'Tis brain, not skin nor hair, that makes the man.

Call us aliens? We, aliens? The people who were the foundation of the American civilization, aliens? A people who, by their sweat, assisted in clothing the barren rocks of the Northeast in verdure, who drained the swamps of the South, and made them to mimic gold in harvest time; who, by their endurance, toil and suffering, made it possible for our white neighbors to establish this government, the asylum of us all; who, by their toil, established the canal and railroad systems of this country—call us aliens? Then to whom can the term citizens *be applied?*

A residence of our foreparents of near three hundred years; birth and rearage here; our adaptation to the wants of the country; our labor and forbearance; our loyalty to the government—are all these the elements indices of an alien race? If we are aliens, then who are the citizens? It is true that we did not come here of our own volition, nor is the epoch of our coming one to be remembered with delight. There was no Castle Garden open to us; no Christian mission inviting us to come; but against our will, in chains, we were dragged from our native land to assist in converting the wilds of America into homes of freemen; to assist in establishing this government, the best that has ever been given to man. Its foundations were laid by our toil and sufferings; its growth and development have been matured by our blood. Whether on the farms, in the workshops, the canals, the railroads or in your homes—wherever work was to be done, obstacles overcome and barren hills to be fertilized—there, at all times, the white man could rely upon the Negro, and he has never failed him.

The Negro has borne the burden of toil, and for what? To plan a civilization from which he is to be forever excluded. No, no, no! We have purchased it with labor; we have purchased it with afflictions; we have purchased it with loyalty; we have purchased it with blood drawn at the point of the lash of the taskmaster; we have purchased it with blood spilt upon the fields of battle; it is ours by all the laws of right and justice. Right, under the watchful care of God, makes might. It is ours, absolutely ours. We are no more alien to this country or to its institutions than our brothers in white. We have instituted it; our forefathers paid dearly for it. The broken hearts of those who first landed here is the first price that was paid for the blessings for which we now contend. By the God of right, by the God of justice, by the God of love, we will stay here and enjoy it, share and share alike with those who call us aliens and invite us to go. Together, we planted the tree of liberty and watered its roots with our tears and blood, and under its branches, we will stay and be sheltered.

Mr. President, those of you who seek to deny us this boon of citizenship tell the North a tale of woe and say that good government and white supremacy are in danger, and to protect the sweets of domestic happiness that were bequeathed us by our fallen sires, white and Black, it is necessary to disfranchise the Negro. Shades of these departed heroes, be witness to what I here say: The Negro does not by his presence retard the wheels of progress. The Negro will never by his vote overthrow good government. The Negro will never by any act of his seek to destroy white supremacy. He is nonobstructive; he is the best element of conservative citizenship of the South. Into his hands is the keeping of peace and happiness of the Southern people.

But the Honorable George D. Tillman [the brother of Benjamin] *says the South is a conquered province. The majority of you blame the poor Negro for the humility inflicted upon you during that conflict, but he had nothing to do with it. It was your love of power and your supreme arrogance that brought it upon yourselves. You are too feeble to settle up with the government for that old grudge. The hatred has been centered upon the Negro; and he is the innocent sufferer of your spleen. But, sirs, we are here. We intend to obey every phase of law that you may legislate against us. We intend to continue to love and forgive you for what you are doing to us. We intend to remain here and cause the South to blossom anew with our toil and suffering. We intend to place our case in the hands of God and the American white people, and while we are waiting for the full enjoyment for the blessings about which Jefferson wrote, for which Washington fought and Attucks died, let me remind you of the truism that the part is not greater than the whole, and we know that we are compelled* to move along within our circumscribed limits until the majority of the white sons and daughters of the South, yea, the entire nation, shall cease to be fooled into the belief that by reason of the Negro's presence, white supremacy is in danger. This is a white man's country, it is claimed, and I will not discuss it, but let me recall to you the words of the sainted Lincoln: "You can fool all of the people sometimes, you can fool some of the people some of the time, but you can't fool all of the people all of the time."

The flame of education is ablaze and sheds its rays from every hilltop and amid the dales, and through and by means of education the scales of prejudice and false impressions will fall from the scales of every White man, high and low. And they, right here in the South, will in time accord us every right and shed blood by our sides to maintain it. But to say that we are not fitted to enjoy the rights of a voter at this time is false, absolutely false, for we are the conservative element of Southern citizenship.

Senator Tillman, in an interview a few days ago, said that the Southern white man is the true friend of the Negro, and he asked the North to keep out of this discussion and deliver the rights of Negro citizenship to his proffered, tender mercy. I would not deny that the Southern white man is friendly to the Negro and will and does assist him as long as he does not attempt to don the habiliments of American citizenship, but if he attempts to clothe himself in the garb of citizenship and claim equal rights before the law under the Stars and Stripes, the average white man becomes cantankerous, and he imagines things that are impossible, and if he chances to be a leader, he flaunts into the face of the American nation the false flag of the fear of Negro domination. The Negroes do not want to dominate. They do not want and would not have social equality, but they do want to cast a ballot for the men who make the laws and administer the laws.

Is there anything new in this plaintive appeal to the nation, asking in the name of friendship for and to the Negro to be left with the Negro and his rights in their hands? Why, sirs, it is not, for it was the cry of the feudal lords when they were grinding the white slaves of Europe between the millstones of misery and poverty. It was the cry of the school of slavery when the chains of servitude were riveted around the necks of the slaves on this continent, and the thoughtful are always reminded that when the lords of the soil ask the common people to surrender to them their rights, whether the intention is so to do or not, they are building barriers between people who surrender to them their rights.

This reminds me that here on this floor, in the discussion of the rights of man, the delegate from Richland, Mr. Patton, though a very shoot of the lost cause, echoes the dying wall of intended servitude, and prefaced his remarks by saying that he was a student of the Bible, and for that reason, he believed in human slavery and said that the words of the sacred writer, "Servants, obey your masters," carried with it the truth that God intended and did not make one race inferior to the other races for the sole purpose of sustaining a slaveholding class.

I do not blame the young gentleman for the assertion of his belief, because from his discussion of that subject his ignorance of ethnology is patent, or he sleeps in blissful disregard of the condition of mankind and their environments when the sacred writer said in the domain of the Roman empire, "Servants, obey your masters." Let me remind the gentleman and every other man in the South or North, that the words "Servants, obey your masters" had no application to the Negro race, for the historians of Rome say that their slavery was white slavery. History records that it was the slaves sent from Gaul were the Teutons, and the slaves who were sent back to Rome from England were the Anglos. I remind that proud Caucasian that on the soil of South Carolina, in that city of Charleston, Anglo-Saxon women were sold as galley slaves by white men. Now, which one of us here today, mixed as badly as I am between Negro and white, or claiming to be as pure in the Anglo-Saxon blood as the gentleman form Richland, can lay our hands upon the Bible and swear that our blood is not mixed with the blood of those white women who were sold as slaves in the city of Charleston? Then sir, with this curse of slavery inflicted upon all the races in every stage of the existence of the human family, we cannot twist the phrase "Servants, obey your masters" to mean the degradation of any particular race or clan of the human family. It surely had no application to the Negro when uttered.

In the image of God, made He man, all equal, in the possession of inalienable rights, but at all times, it has been the property-owning class who have sought to grind down, impoverish and brutalize their own blood if that blood was in the body of the poor and the weak. It is against class legislation that I stand here and raise my voice, and in the name of the poor, struggling white man and the peaceful, toiling, loving Negro. I ask that this act of feudal barbarism against the poor and common people do not be engrafted into and become a part of the Magna Carta of free white and Black South Carolinians.

Mr. President, it is the boast that no illiterate white man shall be disfranchised. It is the boast that the illiterate and educated poor Negro shall be disfranchised. Pass this law, and you shall disfranchise both, unless trickery and fraud are to be enthroned at our voting booths. Pass this law, and you disfranchise all the laboring people, white and Black, unless you so administer this law, which is the avowed intention of your leaders, as to discriminate against the Negro. Such a discrimination, Mr. President, will be a nullification of the Fifteenth Amendment. In the thirties, our statesmen played at the game of nullification, and ever thereafter, they taught nullification until their teachings culminated in secession and secession led to war, and a brother's hand was imbued in a brother's blood in that fight which was the struggle of the common people against the slaveholding class; the common people won that fight, and hence, by reason of false teaching, and by South Carolina's placing her interests in the hands of selfish and ambitious men in the past, we are in this deplorable condition. Right is right, because God is God. Let us, as sons of South Carolina, dare to do right to all our citizens, for it is the only safe course of our citizens or state to follow. Therefore, I do hope that the enacting words of the articles of disfranchisement will be stricken out. It is hard to kick against the pricks. The majority of the white people of this nation are of the common, laboring class, and they will not sit down idly and see South Carolina again nullify any law that secures to the common people rights that are sacred to every freeman.

In the thirties, our politicians were warned by [James] *Petigru, and that master of orators Thomas S. Grimke, of the dangers that lay in their way while they were marching on the road to nullification. But they would not heed the words of warning, and they followed the teachings of that misguided statesman, John. C. Calhoun.*

Oh! Countrymen, there is no good to come of this state out of this proposed act. Let us kill it and return to the constitutional provisions that we now have relating to the subject. I would that you could see the future as I see it. I would that our statesmen would use their energies and their great brain development in a better cause. I would that they would formulate plans by which our waste places could be reclaimed. Labor to bring immigrants into the confines of the dear old state. Strive to induce capital to come into our midst. Strive to teach the masses the lessons to forbear and stand the ills we have and ask God to assist us in a united effort, with one true purpose, and that purpose to make South Carolina the home of the free, loving prosperous humanity. Labor, let us all, to banish from our state caste prejudice and hatred of one man toward another. Let us cease to legislate in favor of any class of people. Let us tell our people that this is the common heritage of whites and Blacks, and it is our duty as free men to live in peace and assist in the government of the state.

Let our labor to prove that we are all a part of this nation, that we love her and intend to make this part of our common country the most glorious and certain place for peace and happiness of any portion of our great domain.

Mr. President, about ten years ago, or maybe less, I chanced to be in the city of Charleston, and the sun was about to set in the west. I strolled from my home to the Citadel Square and seated myself on one of those seats viewing the grand scenery that surrounded me. While there, I beheld a typical Southern gentleman of infirm age approaching me. Running by him was a fair maiden of about eight or nine summers. She was rolling a hoop and just in front of my seat, she stopped as if she had received a deadly blow. She cast her eyes in the direction of the object I had been studying. She exclaimed, "Oh Grandpapa, what great, big, graveyard stone is that? Who has been buried there," she continued, "since we have been in the country?" The old gentleman reached out his hands, trembling as if palsied and drew this winsome little tot to his embrace. He struggled to clear his voice. Tears began to sparkle in his eyes. Said he, "Grandpapa's little jewel has innocently called that pile of stone and bronze a great big graveyard stone, and you are not far out of the way. And if you will listen, I will tell you a tale unfold."

The little girl, looking into her grandfather's face, saw the great big drops of tears that fell upon his spotless linen. Said he: "When your mama was a girl like yourself and your papa was a rambling youth, there was a giant in intellect by the name of John C. Calhoun. He taught us that the state was greater than the nation. That it was our right to disobey the laws of this nation. That it was our right to withdraw from the nation and it was our sacred privilege to do as we pleased. At that time, your grandmother had over thirty servants in the house and hundreds of Negroes on our plantations. We were rich, haughty, proud, refined, virtuous and cultured. With a heart full of hope and a hand ready to dare and do, Calhoun's teachings led us to war, and the bones of our sons are scattered upon every battlefield from Gettysburg to the banks of the Mississippi. In that struggle, our hopes were crushed, our homes were burned, our prosperity destroyed and our servants freed. And, my dear little tot, since you have called that magnificent monument that the women have erected to John C. Calhoun a great, big, *graveyard stone and have asked who is buried there, I am forced to admit that it is a huge, graveyard stone under which is buried a people's blind ambition; under which is buried the hearts and hopes of all your kindred; under which is buried all that was dear to the hearts of the Southern man. And those of us who are left are compelled to stand the wreck of fortune and spend our old days in misery, poverty and want."*

Oh! How long shall the South, through her shortsighted leaders, continue to legislate against the principles for which our forefathers came to this wilderness. It is useless to ask the ministers of the gospel to teach us the lesson of the Nazarene, "Do unto others as you would have them do unto you." For if they should come, we would receive them not. But I do look towards the future with the hope of a better day for both races, but that better day will be only at hand when we shall have been taught that simple command, "Father, let thy will be done," and do unto others that which you would have them do unto you."

Miller concluded his lengthy address that evening with the following anecdote, which summed up the real reasons behind the convention.

Now, Mr. President, I am nearly through, but I cannot stop without asking why is there no minority report from the suffrage committee. We have here the white people of the state divided into two bitter factions. For short, I will call them the "outs" and the "ins." On the committee of suffrage, the "outs" had their brightest jewels, Mr. Hutson, Mr. Bryan, and Mr. McGowan. The "ins" or Tillmanites had their best brain, and at the head of their suffrage committee is their great chieftain and leader, Senator B.R. Tillman. The extreme of the white factions met on that committee, and if there was not some bamboozling done, there would have been two reports. Somebody has been bamboozled, somebody has been outgeneraled, whether he knows it or not. The "outs" or conservatives are satisfied. They have secured all they want, for the committee's report disfranchises the poor common white man who does not own $300 worth of property. The conservatives are rich, and they are satisfied. To illustrate the position of the conservatives on that committee of this convention, I will relate a fish story.

In Colleton County a white lad was crossing the Salkehatchie [River], and in the black water stream, he saw a huge, copper-belly, black back moccasin more than eight feet long. A little ways off, he saw a war-mouth catfish more than three feet long. All of a sudden, the catfish made for the moccasin, and the moccasin went for the cat. The cat began to swallow the moccasin at the end of his tail, and the moccasin began to swallow the catfish. There was powerful swallowing done. The boy stood there until the cat had swallowed the moccasin halfway and the moccasin had swallowed the catfish up to the fin on the back, and they both began to grunt and squirm. The boy concluded that they would both die, and he ran home to his father and said, "Pa, I seen the durndest piece of swallowing you ever heard tell of. A great big copper-belly, black back moccasin more than eight feet long swallowing a three-foot catfish, and Pa, that catfish was swallowing the moccasin. I left them choking and dying. The catfish will die from suffocation, and the moccasin will die from strangulation!" The father said, "Well son, if you ain't fibbing, we will see that there catfish and snake in the morning, but they won't be dead, for they are hard things to die!"

After the hearty laughter of the convention, Miller finished his speech with this explanation that ended with more laughter from the delegates.

To illustrate, the catfish is the conservatives, or "outs," and the moccasin is the Tillmanites, or "ins." When the old man got there in the morning, the snake and the catfish were still swallowing and grunting. Only the head of the catfish was out. His great fin had passed the mouth of the moccasin. All at once, there was a tremendous struggle, and the catfish turned completely around inside the moccasin, and in turning, the fin of the catfish cut the windpipe of the moccasin. There was a little blood seen, and the moccasin died. In this instance, the blood that the catfish drew from this monstrosity, as Senator Irby calls it, the suffrage scheme by which the Negro and poor white man are disfranchised. The moccasin is dead. The catfish is alive. For they are rich, and they will under this act return to power. There is no need for a minority report, because the catfish has killed the moccasin.[21]

The accompanying article noted that Miller was "attentively listened to," but was interrupted only once when Mr. Patton of Richland County rose to correct a statement attributed to him regarding race and the Bible. Miller would resume his defense, as stated below, on October 31 and November 2, 1895.

The gentleman from Edgefield [Benjamin Tillman] *has read from the* Book of Fraud *to prove that my race is not qualified to vote, and why so? Is he ignorant of the way in which the book was made up? If he from experience knew so much about it as I do, he would not quote from it so freely. It was prepared by a partisan committee, and it is greatly colored.*

But, Mr. President, I will not discuss that threat-worn tale so eloquently rehashed by the two gentlemen form Edgefield [Messrs. Tillman and Sheppard], *but I do remind them and this convention that the white people of South Carolina themselves are responsible for the state of affairs which existed during what they call "the dark period of their struggle," than is the Negro or carpetbagger. Though they had been in rebellion, seeking to destroy the very foundation of the greatest government ever planned and maintained, Congress by humane and charitable acts made it possible for them and the Negroes as coheirs to reconstruct their own state governments; but with a haughtiness that showed their contempt for favors bestowed, they stood aloof, refused to vote or assist in reconstructing what in mad folly they had destroyed.*

A new class of rulers called carpetbaggers came among the ignorant Negroes, some of them honest and with patriotic motives. The country had been desolated by five years of war. County jails and courthouses had been destroyed, bridges burned, ferries broken up and roads cut to pieces— all of which had to be reconstructed. Charitable and penal institutions had to be rebuilt and maintained, and city, village and town governments reestablished, making this period peculiarly adapted to speculation, jobbery and plunder. Is it to be wondered at that right on the heels of a great war, with so much to be done anew, there was jobbery and speculation? There were many avenues to be traversed, great and diversified work to be done, and it was therefore impossible to keep out of the administration of affairs men who came among us to plunder. Why continue to hold that picture up to prove the worthlessness of a race? Removed so far as we are from it, why continue to say that by reason of such acts, we should not be entrusted with the right to vote?

Strange as it may appear, I plead specially for the Negro; during the three years he was a major factor in making and sustaining the government in South Carolina, that is from 1873 to 1876, he displayed greater conservative force, appreciation for good laws, knowledge of the worth of honest financial legislation, regard for the rights of his fellow citizens in relation to property and aptitude for honest financial state legislation than has ever been shown by any other people. "Fresh from the auction block and the slave pen," in the words of Professor Bryce, "ten-year-old children were more fitted to exercise the franchise." They first elected whom they supposed to be their friends, but in the short period of less than five years, we who participated in that government learned that though they were our friends, any act on their part predicated upon plunder meant universal destruction, and from 1873 to 1876, inclusive, the record made by Negro legislators and Negroes charged with fiduciary trusts in the management of the government for certain reforms, has never been surpassed in any of the conservative states of New England. It is but too true, "the evil one does lives after him—the good is oft interred with his bones."

We were eight years in power. We had built schoolhouses, established charitable institutions, built and maintained the penitentiary system, provided for the education of the deaf and dumb, rebuilt the jails and courthouses, rebuilt the bridges and reestablished the ferries. In short, we had reconstructed the state and placed it upon the road to prosperity and, at the same time, by our acts of financial reform, transmitted to the Hampton government an indebtedness not greater by more than $2,500,000 than was the bonded debt of the state before 1868, before the Republican Negroes and their white allies came into power.

I stand here pleading for justice to a people whose rights are about to be taken away with one fell swoop, and I don't stand here answering any personal allusions, but representing the interests of the most conservative element of the Southern citizenship.

What is the trouble? The trouble comes from this, Mr. President. One white faction in South Carolina has been arrayed against another, and to prevent us from standing up in a representative capacity in a minority as representatives of the majority, they have rehashed this stale tale that has been written and read by the North, East and West until judgment has been passed upon it.[22]

The conclusion of Miller's message was printed in the *Columbia State* on November 2, 1895.

Because there had been robbery and fraud and perjury during a part of the time of Negro domination as it is called, it must not be thought that all Negroes were dishonest any more than that all white men in New York were dishonest because Tweed and his gang had been corrupt. That did not signify that all of the men who put Tweed in office were corrupt.

Because white Democrats voted solidly for, and by their votes elected, the most corrupt judge [Thomas J. Mackey] that has ever disgraced the judicial ermine in South Carolina, why should the white people of our state be pronounced as venal as that arch scoundrel?

Oh, Mr. President, peace! Peace! Peace is the thing that I ask. But can we hope for peace and good feeling between the two races when such exhibitions as that made here by the gentleman from Edgefield is repeated?

Peace! Peace! Peace, happiness and prosperity and the hope for a brighter day seems withered.

What right would I have to recall the scenes of Hamburg and Ellenton, where the helpless Negroes were murdered in cold blood? What right would I have to refer to the fact that a gentleman on this floor treasures as a parlor ornament a rifle which he claims he used at those riots?

Peace! Peace to all men! Judge these educated white people by what they are doing, and ask them if the poor ignorant Negro should thus be judged.

I want a united people. Let us forever bury all the bad deeds of both races of the past. Let us try to bear and forbear. Let us strive to bind up the wounds, old wounds, of long, long ago, with bandages of loving kindness between the two races. God has placed your race and my race here on this continent; together, it is our lot to dwell. Oh, countrymen, of this Southland, one and all, white and Black, let us be just, one to another; let us at all times speak only the truth about our people and the old state; let us labor to unite our people for the good of the people in common; let us secure to our children prosperity and happiness founded upon the rock of justice and peace, justice and peace, justice and peace![23]

Heartily, even the majority of representatives who would vote to enact the anti-Black elements of the 1895 Constitution applauded this speech. Tillman angrily responded with the "stale tale" that Miller referred to regarding "Negro domination" and corruption during Reconstruction.

Miller's wife, Mary J. Miller, preserved his speeches and the following address in a pamphlet titled *The Suffrage Speeches by Negroes in the Constitutional Convention: The Part Taken by Colored Orators in Their Fight for a Fair and Impartial Ballot.* In her preface, she wrote, "That the country may read these speeches and learn to know these brave and true men, I have edited a few of their arguments and prepared this pamphlet. I regard them as gems of Negro eloquence."[24]

"Chose Ye Whom Ye Will Serve" James Wigg's Appeal

According to historian Lawrence S. Rowland in the *South Carolina Encyclopedia*, James Wigg was born in Beaufort County in slavery around 1850. During his boyhood, the Union army occupied Hilton Head Island, and Union general David Hunter took young Wigg to Washington, D.C., where he was educated at the Whalen Institute. After he served as a delegate to the constitutional convention, little appears about him in the public record, although the website Ancestry.com reports that a James Wigg of Beaufort, who would have been about the same age as the convention delegate, died of dysentery on September 15, 1916. His remarks were made after Thomas Miller's initial address on October 25, 1895.[25]

Mr. President, there can be no issue of greater importance than the suffrage. We are now face to face with a problem of tremendous importance to each one of us and all of our constituents. If you meet the issue dispassionately, patriotically and honestly, and honestly, with an eye single to the public good, you will render the state a service that will endure for ages to come, and unborn generations will rise and call you blessed. But if in a spirit of passion and caste, you elect to turn a deaf ear to the voice of reason and experience and blindly arrogate yourselves rights that you do not justly possess, striving to turn backward on the dial of time the shadow that makes the advancement of liberty and equal rights, you will be guilty of a tremendous blunder and will ruthlessly reopen issues long since thought to be closed and wounds which good people everywhere hoped had been healed.

You are now considering the keystone to your political arch—the suffrage. Whatever errors you may make in the structure must be corrected in the suffrage—if it be corrected at all. Therefore, Mr. President, it behooves you to build wisely—to select your materials with the utmost care, so that when you leave this place, you may go with no misgivings of ill, nor retributions to come.

Those of you who have allowed yourselves to be deluded by fear of a possible "Negro domination," as opposed to what you are pleased to call "white supremacy," are largely responsible for the conditions existing. You have summoned before the Bar of the people of South Carolina and before the country to show cause why the rights guaranteed us by the Fourteenth and Fifteenth Amendments to the federal Constitution should be annulled and made of none effect.

You have declared your intention to solve for South Carolina the so-called Negro problem and to sever at a single stroke the Gordian knot of the suffrage by disfranchising as many Negroes as possible, so as to make it impossible for him by any force of circumstances of wealth or intelligence to outvote the white people and control the destinies of the state.

White supremacy, you say, must be secured, by honest means if you can, by dishonest means if you must. This, I believe, every white delegate here stands pledged. Beneath this yoke, humiliating as it is, each one of you had to pass; to this pledge, each one of you had to subscribe before you could have the privilege of being counted as a delegate to this convention.

The doctrine so persistently taught that the interests of the Negro and Anglo Saxon are so opposed as to be irreconcilable is a political subterfuge; a fallacy so glaring in its inception, so insulting to Providence, so contrary to reason and logic of history, that one can scarcely refrain from calling in question either the sanity or honesty of its advocates.

The edict has gone forth that for the preservation of white supremacy, the Negro must be disfranchised to such an extent that it shall be forever impossible for him to outvote his white brother, whether he shall exceed him in intelligence or not. To accomplish this result, you are urged to trample underfoot every law, human or divine, to set at defiance every Christian and patriotic sentiment which honorable men are accustomed to hold dear.

Mr. President, Providence has seen fit, for reasons beyond our ken, to place side by side in South Carolina two races of men—two brothers, if you please—who, like Cain and Abel, seem to be pursuing different occupations and inclinations, one white, the other Black. The one owning most of the soil, and from long years of unjust mastery, arrogant, impatient of restraint and domineering. The other, owning but little of the soil, but having an intense attachment for the place of his birth, docile, easily contented, law abiding and industrious. Both of these brothers are citizens of a common country, children of one mother, South Carolina. Each one of them rendering services to their common parent and each owing filial obedience to her laws. Neither can justly claim services which can be denied to the other. Both of them have shed their blood in their country's service and have fought side by side upon a hundred battlefields, from the first skirmish on Boston Commons, when Crispus Attucks fell, to the Battle of New Orleans, when the flower of the British army faded before the leaden storms from Black battalions under General Andrew Jackson.

That these two races, the whites and the Blacks, are destined to live together can now scarcely be denied. How they may dwell together so that their union shall resound to the best interests of both, and best subserve the good of the state should be the dream not only of Christian philanthropy, but also the highest aim of an enlightened statesmanship and worthy of the very best thought of which you are capable. To meet the issue with brute force, to reestablish the doctrine that "might makes right," or to attempt to settle the question among any lines than equal or exact justice to all will fall as it ought.

The Negro, Mr. President, has a right to demand that in accordance with his wealth, his intelligence and his services to the state, he be accorded an equal and exact share in his government. This is his just due: he asks no more, he will accept no less. That the state has the right to make any qualification of the suffrage which shall operate justly and equally among all who will desire to enter late citizenship hereafter, I admit freely. But sir, I do deny with all the strength of which I am capable the right of the state to abridge the rights of the citizen now a voter, either directly or indirectly.

You charge that the Negro is too ignorant to be trusted with the suffrage. I answer that you have not, nor dare you, make a purely educational test of the right to vote. You say that he is a figurehead, an incumbrance to the state, that he pays little to no taxes. I answer you, you have not, and you dare not, make a pure property test of the right to vote, Mr. President, for ignorance and poverty to rule wealth and intelligence is a monstrosity, but for intelligence and wealth to seize upon the citadel of power and hedge in poverty and ignorance with impossible conditions of advancement is a crime.

Another phase of the Negro problem: for over thirty years, the Negro has been meeting and refuting every charge made against him. Quietly and peaceably, he has lived among you. Beset on all sides with laws unjustly administered, by lynch laws and mob laws, he has preserved the peace and dignity of the state with a patience unparalleled in the history of the world. He has neither attempted by plots to overthrow the government, nor by strikes to imperil your prosperity. He has waited with patience, content to bide his time when his white brothers' sense of justice will permit him, without rioting or bloodshed, to enjoy the rights guaranteed to him by the constitution and laws of this country.

The edict has gone forth that the Negro must be disfranchised to such an extent that it will be impossible for him to ever outvote his white brother, whether he shall excel him in intelligence or not. To accomplish this result, you are urged to trample under foot every law, human or divine, to set at defiance every Christian and patriotic sentiment which honorable men are instructed to hold dear.

We are told that the Mississippi plan will do the work. The distinguished gentleman from Edgefield has distinctly declared that the law must bear upon its face the impress of fairness and justice, but white supremacy must be secured by the execution of the law. In plain words, you are told that on account of the two amendments to the federal Constitution and honest qualification of the suffrage which will ensure what they call white supremacy, with honest safeguards for individual rights is impossible. But you must surrender to whomever occupies the executive office all those safeguards, which a thousand years of experience and struggle have found imperative for the security of individual rights.

The committee offers you white supremacy with white degradation. We offer you the supremacy of law, intelligence and property. "Choose ye whom ye will serve." Will you make justice, honor, law, fidelity and the truth the palladium of your liberties, or will you make injustice, perjury and fraud the foundation of your policy? We have pled our cause. If you refuse to adjudicate our claims, we will yield to the inevitable, but we shall appeal from Phillip drunk to Phillip sober. We submit our case to the judgement of an enlightened public opinion, and to the advancement of a Christian civilization.[26]

"Justice Cannot Sleep Forever" William J. Whipper's Plea

Whipper's orations, unlike those he made at the 1868 Convention, read as among the most passionate of the speeches from the 1895 Convention. In the middle of the address, he spoke to the verbal abuse these men faced during the 1895 Convention. The newspaper accounts from the *Columbia State* and *Charleston News and Courier* confirm the frequent racial slurs and rudeness to the Black delegates, occasionally by the newspapers themselves. This speech was given at the convention on October 26, 1895, and published in the next day's edition of the *Columbia State*.

Mr. President: In the course of human events, especially in Democratic governments, it becomes necessary to call what is known as constitutional conventions. When so called, if the people are consulted, their wishes, properly ascertained, it becomes a body on the highest pinnacle of authority, with great powers, powers above all others; above the judiciary, which it creates; above the legislature, for which it lays down the rules to be governed by; above the executive. Indeed, it is the highest pinnacle of power that the people can place their representatives upon. This was true no matter whether the convention had been properly called or not. I will suppose for the purpose of this argument that it has been properly called.

When there, with those extraordinary powers, their duty is to look up through the corridors of time to the star of immutable justice and fix the dial of organic law upon the same, so that in coming legislatures in the future may be governed and ruled thereby, as well as the judiciary and the executive. Whether or not this is such a body, I stop not here to inquire. Suffice it to know that we so represent ourselves to the world. If this is not our purpose, we must then have a wicked purpose.

Now to the bill before us, which I am compelled to characterize as a snare, a subterfuge, a delusion. The only thing in connection with it is the fact that its authors declared six months or more before the calling of this convention that it was necessary to disfranchise the Negro without disfranchising a single white man. Why should the Negro be thus outraged, wronged, robbed, defrauded of his franchise? Do not the white people, North and South, owe him a debt of lasting gratitude?

Does the bill say these people are to be left out? The purpose was avowed with frankness some months before. They had stated that they intended to call the convention to disfranchise the Negro. Now should the Negro be disfranchised? If so, it ought to be done in an open and frank manner, and not by the subterfuge in this article. When suffrage was conferred on the Negro, he was not fit to exercise it. But there were many white men in the same condition. It was a mistake. The Negro was led away by the superior race. I have been here 31 days and have heard them try to prove you are the superior race. We admit that. We were just out of the bondages of slavery and ignorance. You have culture. You have had schools and colleges—all open to you. The doors of these have been closed to us. We concede your superiority, and it is little to boast of. Wait 30 years and see how the Negro advances. We concede that the Negro was unprepared for the ballot when he got it. For 235 years, all efforts were directed to the training of the Negro's muscles. The white man was equally unfit. One class had been ignorant, the others had been taught the Negro was the basis of property. The Negro was at the bottom of the bloody war. Their bitterness made them unfit doing justice to the Negro. You will find all this in the Black Code passed by the whites in 1865. Time has proven they were not qualified to take the ballot offered to them. They passed this miserable code. Three years, it existed under the bayonet.

Well, we may look back to those days to see what results came. We know not whether there will be another Reconstruction. This was what brought about the Reconstruction Acts of 1868. They had been discussed here with a freedom that was sometimes disgusting. In 1868, they passed the Reconstruction Acts. When the whole field was open, there was not a white man who wanted to come out and guide the inferior, ignorant race, and Negroes were ushered into that constitutional convention. I refer to it with pride, for it gave you the best constitution under which you have ever lived. If that was not so, then why have you lived under it for all these years? The people of the North and South owed to that convention a great deal of gratitude.

During the war, when the clouds hung like a pall under the federal forces, when reserve after reserve gave encouragement and made it to appear that the Confederacy would succeed, when General Lee marched within a few miles of the capital of Pennsylvania, Abraham Lincoln and his advisors felt that it was necessary to call upon the Negro. He came forward and readily took up arms, and before the war ended, 186,000 Negroes marched to the thread of martial music—186,000 Negroes exposed themselves to the bayonets, cannons and musketry of the Confederacy, and they largely assisted in hurling it to its grave. Nor is this all; they assisted as pioneers at building forts, wagon drivers and, above all, there was confidential bearers of confidential messages, upon which our greatest generals acted in the most critical moments. He was a sturdy and valuable guide. This shows you the debt that the federal side owes us.

I now turn to the other side. Gentlemen, there is a debt you owe us. There was the horny-handed laborer, the bread winner of the Confederacy, remaining at home caring for the family of the master, working the plantation, discharging every duty, protecting those who were most dear to those who were fighting the battles of the Confederacy. His loyalty was unquestioned, either by the Union forces or by the Confederacy, no matter with what he was entrusted. This is a brief outline of the debt of gratitude that both parties owe to the Negro. But there is more that he has done for you since 1620. His arm has laid your forests, tilled your soil, built your railroads, and yet he is the party you are here to defraud. We are not here, I say it with all earnestness, in the attitude of beggars. I am not begging but asking the right to which the Negro is entitled. There were evils so far as wealth was concerned. They were inferior, but such superiority should not be shown in this way. This isn't the place to show that you are superior by defrauding the Negro race—your devoted old slaves.

This is the Negro who by this bill is proposed to disfranchise. And why? Because you say he was not qualified to be a voter? I grant that when the Reconstruction Acts were passed, he was not so qualified. It was a necessity created by the people of South Carolina themselves. Andrew Johnson, in his desire to have the states restored, gave to them the greatest latitude, and it was the adoption of the Black Code and the ordinances of the Convention of 1865, which placed the Negro in a condition almost as bad as slavery itself that made it necessary for the United States government to devise some plan to protect the freedman, the wards of the nation. That it was a mistake to clothe him with the elected franchise, it is true. It is just as great a mistake to clothe the southern white man with that inestimable boon. The Negro was unfit for it in consequence of his ignorance, which ignorance was enforced upon him. The feeling of the white man toward the Negro at that time was such as thoroughly to unfit him to mete out justice to them, to or even to enact laws in accord with the spirt of the times, as shown in the ordinances of the South Carolina Convention of 1865 and the Black Code of 1865, which I now hold in my hand, which, pardon me, I do not mean to read.

The *Columbia State* then noted that Whipper gestured while holding up the papers containing these laws by holding them upward as he made his points.

I pass from this. It is also claimed that the Negro is an inferior race. I grant it. It would be a high compliment to slavery and oppression that with thirty years of freedom, the Negro is the equal to the white man, who has had the advantage of two hundred years of American civilization and countless centuries of English civilization. Who has had trained and educated mothers and grandmothers to rear them as statesmen, philosophers, artisans, etc., to grapple with the new ideas of the world. Schoolhouses open to them everywhere, from the county schoolhouse at the crossroads to Edinburgh and Heidelberg on the other side of the ocean and Yale and Harvard on this side, while all the avenues of learning and education have been closed against the Negro and are only yielding now to his indomitable will and that too chiefly in the northern states.

I am not here as a suppliant, nor do I put myself and my race in the attitude of a beggar. I am here as a man and a representative, not representing simply the Negro, but representing the people. The fact that I am a Negro has nothing to do with my status here. And just here, I will digress to speak of the flippant way the term nigger *has been used in this convention. I am a Negro. There are five others here that are Negroes. We are proud of it, and we hope to be able to do something in and out of this convention that the Negroes will be proud of and white men compelled to recognize. But when men selected from their various counties, as it is fair to suppose with a view to their intelligence and their good standing at their various homes, assemble there with the responsibility resting upon them can so flippantly use the word niggers, spelt with two Gs, it is hurtful, and I feel it keenly. It stings sharper than a serpent's tooth when it comes from the venerable gentleman from Edgefield, Mr. George D. Tillman, whom I have learned to respect, not simply on account of his age, but for his gentlemanly deportment. In a heated contest lasting for days and nights, where eye looked into eye and voice to voice, he responded without an unpleasant word, but here through the word* nigger, *he used with a flippancy that is painful to us all.*

The other gentleman from Edgefield, Mr. Benjamin R. Tillman, by his constant use of the word, would lead one to suppose he had a small Negro in his boots or pantaloons or somewhere in close touch with him all the time. I don't wish it to be understood or go out into the world that we have received this treatment from all the delegates here, or even from a majority of them, but I cannot avoid resenting it from whom it does come. Whilst we as delegates must submit to it, we regret to feel that it comports with their idea of gentility. Can you be proud of this? Tower above the Negro. Climb higher up the ladder of fame. When I find men trying to hold men down instead of lifting them up, it grieves me.

Is the Negro such a bad citizen that you should violate all law, human and divine, and chain him down? You have the wealth and intelligence. Now you say you mustn't let the Negro vote because he will vote against you. The Negro is an imitative being. This has made him valuable and a necessity. What the Negro asks now is that they be treated as men. You say that you must rule the country; that it is the white man's country. We are here to ask you to stay your hand and do justice.

When the gentleman from Barnwell comes here and labors long to show that under the Fifteenth Amendment that the Negroes were not entitled to hold office, I say, wasn't that a small effort. If the Negro wasn't fit, how could he hold office? Another gentleman—even here in the evening of the nineteenth century—comes and says the Bible justified slavery. He says he would like to have one hundred slaves now. If he had them, he would be worse off than any one of you. He would be taught that his business was unprofitable and troublesome.

We have only 6 of us here of the inferior race, and you have 154. Men upon this floor are clamoring for white supremacy, come here and assume dignity, and call us "niggers" with the flippancy of barroom attendants. The trouble here is "Negro rule" and "white supremacy." Was there ever any such thing as "Negro rule" in South Carolina? It was the rule of white men supported by the Negroes. Aren't there more Negroes than white men on your farms? Yet doesn't your wife rule? In the Convention of 1868, there were less than a dozen Negroes and less than a dozen white men engaged in the work done there. I am proud of the work done in that convention. The way, it has stood the test has shown that there was nothing dangerous in it. They had simply taken the best parts of other constitutions. Most of the men were there to vote as they were told.

This convention, 'tis said, is to prevent Negro rule and establish white supremacy. Again, as a matter of fact, there was never any Negro rule in South Carolina. When was there ever a time when we had a Negro governor? We never had a majority of Negro officers at any time in this state. Indeed, there were only four colored men who ever held any of the state offices and that only for a single term each. There was never a county in this state controlled by colored officers. In fact, all of the important officers, clerk of court, sheriff, treasurer, auditors throughout the state, with less than a half dozen exceptions, have been filled by white men. Does this look like Negro rule? Even in the darkest hours of Reconstruction, where the bad legislation led to the fall of the Republican Party, white men held the offices, white men did the robbery, many of them Democrats of the deepest dye, who reaped the rewards for their purchase of Negroes. There never was a Negro lobbyist parading the corridors of this house. They were white men. Call them carpetbaggers, scalawags, renegades, what you will, they were white men and are responsible for the bad legislation. Charge this not up to the account of the Negro. There was never a time in even old Beaufort County where there were not more white officers than Negroes. Is that Negro rule?

Beaufort never had a colored sheriff during the Reconstruction period. Talk about Negro rule. The Negro could have ruled, but he has never shown discretion. There was never Negro rule in a single county or a single town in this state. I ask the body, was there a town with a Negro intendant and a majority of the town council? If I am wrong, correct me. We could have elected such in my town of Beaufort. We are twenty to one there. Does this look like Negro rule? Does that look like we want to trample on the rights of the white man?

Do away with this Negro rule howl. When the Negroes had a majority in the lower house, the only place where they ever had a majority, white man governed them. Things were done there that were against his protest—white man ruled. Bonds were flooded all over the state. Corruption was rife. I proclaimed it on the floor. The leading Democratic newspaper in Charleston was even subsidized. That is a matter of record. I warned them to stop. But who were the lobbyists who carried it all through? They were all white men. Some of them South Carolinians, some Democrats from New York. They must take the consequences. White men were in office and controlled the Negro just out of slavery and taking advantage of his weakness. Oh, if the better class of white men had influenced the new freedmen, the necessity for saying all of this would never have existed.

Governor Franklin J. Moses had the swing of that same Charleston newspaper, and it was as silent as the grave and silent for money. That same Charleston paper was subsidized. I can give you the price paid.

According to the *Columbia State*, Representative John Laurens Manning Irby asked Whipper what the name of the newspaper in question was.

I don't remember; it was the News, *I think. I don't think it was the* News *and* Courier *at that time. I can give you the names of the men—[publisher Bartholomew]* Riordan *and [editor Francis Warrington]* Dawson. *The price paid was $5,000. I saw the notes given—and for $2,500 each. I know here those notes are now. They were never paid. Whatever the white man wished, they did; they did it all. I admit the superiority of your race. I want the next gentleman who mentions Negro rule again in this convention to tell me where the Negro did rule. He might have ruled a farm under a white man. Now where does the white man rule? There are now in this country 70,000,000 white men; are they scared of the Negro race? They can't be. Something else must be at the bottom of this. If you do the Negro justice, there's no need to do him harm. To do him injustice changes the situation.*

The Negro never had any power. You simply allowed a different class of white men to manipulate the Negro because you wouldn't. The Negroes are a part of you. Do them justice and there is no need to do what you propose to ensure white supremacy. I believe if this article is adopted, I will live long enough to be a member of another convention. Pass this bill if you dare; and you will call the people of South Carolina to undo the unjust thing you have done. You will make the Negro a nonentity. The Negro has been patient and he will be patient. When you rested in apparent security, owning the Negro himself, there was an influence at work emanating from the throne itself; a situation was brought about that compelled you to do him justice. He was then a slave; you meet him now as a man, and you would strip him of that manhood. I appeal to you to stay that hand and avoid the consequences which will be inevitable. The correction will come. The Negro is here and is here to stay forever. The Negro babies born every day could not be carried off in all the ships you could bring to our shores.

You have work for the Negroes to do; they are here; they are not able to leave and get away. Utilize your uncultivated fields. You need the Negroes, their toil and energy. Instead of toiling to take his ballot away, put him in your fields. You have the capital to utilize in this way. You can trust him now, if only you treat him fair. That he insists upon and will insist upon to the end. Now what is the result of this? The Negro is declared wrong in congress, the Sabbath Schools, etc. What are the results? You find them in mobs, in riots, because of wrongs done him.

In regard to the outrage committed at Hampton a few days ago, this foul murder was the result of such legislation as you intend to impose upon us today. Don't treat the Negro as if he were an alien; for it results in assassination that is rightly turned lynching. I don't want more than justice. In this Hampton case, the victim had been convicted by a white jury, before a judge whom I recently met and had been favorably impressed with. His charge was impressive and fair. I do not know anything about the jury. I will not attempt to what actuated them, the lawyers of the bar or the solicitor. Why was it that they should recommend the victim to mercy? There was evidently some doubt, and they said they would recommend to mercy; we would like to say we have not sent him out of the world. On the way to the place of confinement, these "actors in a play"—resulting from an evil spirit –seized the assassin's knife and plunged it in the man's heart. Such legislation of such bodies as this incited the feeling against the Negro, and hence this crime.

I have spoken nearly two hours. I don't want to tire you. But we are going to make this fight all along the line. I know that nothing I can say will change a single vote. I do say that sooner or later, God being always right, right will eventually prevail. We want you to understand that we have rights, and they must sooner or later be recognized. We are testing the very groundwork of this whole matter in the United States Supreme Court and will push it to the bitter end. We may take it to congress. We want this thing to pass in the very worst form it can pass.

Where township governments exist, we know every rascal in the community. We are now going on with our fight to try to sap the very foundation of this convention. It is a duty I owe to this convention that I tell you this—not in a threatening spirit, however. We go to you now and ask for justice. God is just, and justice cannot sleep forever. I have spoke to you in the kindest of spirit. Whatever concerns mankind, this convention, South Carolina, all these concerns me. Your people today—the Negroes are yours—are deeply concerned.

If you vote down my amendment, then fix the matter in justice to the Negro and to yourselves. Remember ever that the oppressor meets a just fate. Remember too that, "The laws of changeless justice bind oppressor with oppressed, and close as sin and suffering joined, we march to fate abreast."[27]

ROBERT SMALLS ON BLACK VOTING RIGHTS, OCTOBER 26, 1895

This speech followed William Whipper's address that evening.

Mr. President: I have been asked whether I would speak on this important matter. I replied that it all depended on circumstances whether or not I would. The circumstances are such that I have made up my mind to make a short speech on the general bill, and content myself with the vote I will cast on the amendments and sections as they are brought up; inasmuch as I have been perfectly pleased with the speeches made last night, and the one just concluded by the representatives from my county, as I feel that they echo the sentiments not only of the county they represent, but the entire race in the state, and every one I "could claim to represent." I endorse their utterances in the language of Mr. Cash when he said he endorsed "every syllable" and accepted it as his own in this letter. I want to hear some of the speeches on the other side, because I do not like this matter that is called Indian file, as it seems now we are to form a Negro file in this convention. I will only say that this convention has violated the principle laid down in the Constitution under which we are now living, it giving the right for any two members to call for an "aye" and "nay" vote, but the skillful chairman of the committee on rules, from Edgefield, I mean ex-governor—no—I [laughter] has made a rule which requires four above the number we have, to call for the "aye" and "nay" vote, hence we cannot put the members on record without the assistance of some of the white members of the convention. They formed a "dark corner" over there by themselves.

I was born and raised in South Carolina, and today live on the very spot on which I was born, and I expect to remain here as long as the great God allows me to live, and I will ask no one else to let me remain. I love the state as much as any member of this convention, because it is the garden spot of the South.

Mr. President, this convention has been called for no other purpose than the disfranchisement of the Negro. Be careful and bear in mind that the elections which are to take place early next month in very many of the states are watching the action of this convention, especially on the suffrage question. Remember that the Negro was not brought here of his own accord. I found by reference to a history in the Congressional Library in Washington, written by Neil, that he says that in 1619, in the month of June, a Dutch man-of-war landed at Jamestown, Virginia, with fifteen sons of Africa aboard, at the time, Miles Kendall was deputy governor of Virginia. He refused to allow the vessel to be anchored in any of her harbors. But he found out after his order had been sent out that the vessel was without provisions, and the crew was in a starving condition. He countermanded his order and supplied the vessel with the needed provisions in exchange for Negroes. It was then that the seed of slavery was planted in the land. So you see, we did not come here of our own accord; we were brought here in a Dutch vessel, and we have been here ever since. The Dutch are here and are controlling the business of Charleston today. They are not to blame and are not being blamed.

We served our masters faithfully, and willingly, and as we were made to do for 244 years. In the last war, you left them home. You went to the war, fought and came back home, shattered to pieces, worn out, one-legged and found your wife and family being properly cared for by the Negroes you left behind. Why should you now seek to disfranchise a race that has been so true to you?

This Convention has a good leader in the person of the distinguished gentleman from Edgefield. Mr. President, when men are out shooting and want to shoot straight, they are compelled to shut one eye, and this leader uses only one eye in this convention, hence he is always striking the bull's eye; let him beware lest he strikes it one time too often [laughter].

Since Reconstruction times, fifty-three thousand have been killed in the South, and not more than three white men have been convicted and hung for these crimes. I want you to be mindful of the fact that the good people of the earth are watching this convention upon this subject. I hope you will make a constitution that will stand the test. I hope that we may be able to say when our work is done that we have made as good a constitution as the one we are doing away with.

The Negroes are paying taxes in the South on $263,000,000 worth of property. In South Carolina, according to the census, the Negroes pay tax on $12,500,000 worth of property.

That was in 1890. You voted down without discussion merely to lay on the table, a proposition for a simple property and educational qualification. What do you want? You tried the infamous eight-box and registration laws until they were worn to such a thinness that they could stand neither the test of the law nor of public opinion. On behalf of the 600,000 Negroes in the state and the 132,000 Negro voters, all that I demand is that a fair and honest election law be passed. We care not what the qualifications improvised are; all that we ask is that they be fair and honest and honorable, and with these provisions, we will stand or fall by it. You have 102,000 white men over twenty-one years of age; 13,000 of these cannot read nor write. You dare not disfranchise them; and you know that the man who proposes it will never be elected to another office in the state of South Carolina. But whatever Mr. Tillman can do, he can make nothing worse than the infamous eight-box law, and I have no praise for the conservatives, for they gave the people that law. Fifty-eight thousand Negroes cannot read nor write. This leaves a majority of 14,000 white men who can read and write over the same class of Negroes in this state. We are willing to accept a scheme that provides that no man who cannot read nor write can vote, if you dare pass it. How can you expect an ordinary man to "understand and explain" any section of the constitution, to correspond to the interpretation put upon it by the manager of election, when by a very recent decision of the supreme court, composed of the most learned men in the state, two of them put one construction upon a section, and the other justice put an entirely different construction upon it. To embody such a provision in the election law would be to mean that every white man would interpret it aright, and every Negro would interpret it wrong. I appeal to the gentleman from Edgefield to realize that he is not making a law for one set of men. Some morning, you may wake up to find that the bone and sinew of your country is gone. The Negro is needed in the cotton fields and in the low country rice fields, and if you impose too hard conditions upon the Negro in this state, there will be nothing else for him to do but to leave.

What then will you do about your phosphate works? No one but a Negro can work them: the mines that pay the interest on your state debt. I tell you the Negro is the bone and sinew of your country, and you cannot do without him. I do not believe you want to get rid of the Negro, else why did you impose a high tax on immigration agents who might come here to get him to leave?

Now, Mr. President, we should not talk one thing and mean another. We should not deceive ourselves. Let us make a constitution that is fair, honest and just. Let us make a constitution for all the people, one we will be proud of and our children will receive with delight. Don't let us act like a gentleman said he talked. The other day, a gentleman told me that a prominent lawyer, a member of this convention, made a very bitter speech against the Negro while he was a candidate for election to this convention. After the lawyer had concluded his speech of bitterness against the Negro and in favor of white supremacy, some colored men waited on him and asked him why he had made such a bitter speech against them, saying they had regarded the gentleman as their friend, as he had often acted as their lawyer. This gentleman replied to them: "Don't mind my speech. I am a friend to the Negro, but I have got to make bitter speeches to fool the crackers because I want their votes." Gentlemen, I warn you that you can fool the crackers when you talk to them, but if you pass this ordinance that has been proposed by the committee on suffrage, you will fool nobody, for every person in the nation has been informed of your speeches on the stump, and you will not be able to explain it away as that lawyer did his words of bitterness to the colored men who waited on him.

Mr. President, strange things have happened, and I have been shocked in my life, but the greatest surprise of my life was when the distinguished lawyer from Barnwell, Mr. Aldrich, introduced a constitution in this convention that was taken verbatim et literatim from the Constitution of '65 and the Black Code of '66, which deprived every Negro from holding an office in this state, notwithstanding that constitution and Black Code were rejected by Congress. That constitution caused the passage of the acts of Reconstruction by Congress and made it necessary for the Constitutional Convention of 1868, which gave to you the best constitution of any one of the southern states. Let us make a constitution, Mr. President, that will demand the respect of mankind everywhere, for we are not above public opinion. While in Washington, a committee of capitalists came over from England hunting for timber land in which to invest. One of South Carolina's representatives in Congress called upon those gentlemen and informed them that there were large tracts of land in Beaufort County, in the Township of Blufton, for sale. They inquired for the name of the state, and when they were informed that the timber lands were in South Carolina, they answered: "You need not go any further, as our instructions were, before we left England, not to invest money in a state where life and property was not secure under the law." In God's name, let us make a constitution that will receive the approval of everybody—the outside world, as well as those at home.

Some time ago, I heard the distinguished gentleman from Edgefield, I mean Mr. George D. Tillman, say that the white man wanted elbow room, and I suppose that this is what this suffrage plan is proposed to give him. Again, the other day, in this convention, I heard him make a very eloquent speech on the township government bill, but before he got through, he had acted like the good Jersey cow, which gave her two gallons of milk, and, though she did not put her foot in it before she was through, she had shaken so much dirt from her tail into the pail that we could not accept the milk.

Now, Mr. President, I will not detain this convention, as I had no intention of making a speech upon this subject, as I said before; but now, sir, in the language of Mr. E.B. Cash, in his letter received from the distinguished "Bald Eagle" of Edgefield, General Mart Gary [holding up the letter], let me say that I endorse every letter, syllable, verbatim et literatim, and accept as my own the speeches made by my colleagues last night and this morning. And I would, therefore, ask that the convention will not vote down the substitute for the suffrage bill introduced by my colleague, Mr. Whipper, as they did that of Mr. Wigg, by a simple motion to lay on the table, but will allow this matter to go over, as the attendance is very slim, until Monday. I ask the senator from Edgefield if he intends to press this matter to a vote this afternoon.

Senator Tillman remarked that that was what he proposed to do.

Smalls replied, "Ah! I am beginning to know the senator at last. We will be able to shake hands yet if you don't mind."

The *Columbia State* reported that the gathering laughed at this statement but did not say if Tillman and Smalls actually shook hands.[28]

"THE BLOOD OF THE MARTYRS"
ROBERT B. ANDERSON'S WARNING

Robert B. Anderson of Georgetown was born and reared in that county. According to George Tindal's *South Carolina Negroes, 1877–1901*, Anderson served as a schoolteacher, jail warden and, later, a postmaster of Georgetown after serving in the state legislature. He gave his remarks before the convention on October 28, 1895, according to the next day's edition of the *Columbia State* that carried the following speech.[29]

Mr. President and gentlemen of the Constitutional Convention of South Carolina: I arise, sirs, simply to say a few words in favor of the adoption of the substitute offered by the gentleman from Beaufort, General Whipper, in place of the ordinance unanimously reported to this convention by the committee on suffrage for its consideration and adoption.

But sir, it is with a great deal of diffidence that I shall attempt to discuss this subject, for I feel my inability to give justice to a measure so far-reaching in its effect and purpose, a measure that will decide for two decades at least the political destiny of the colored people of South Carolina. But Mr. President, being impelled from sense of stern duty I owe to the people who sent me here—and also on behalf of a million people in my native state—I am constrained to lift my voice in protest against the passage by this convention of the political scheme of suffrage proposed by the committee on suffrage. A scheme that will forever rivet the chain of disfranchisement upon the colored people of South Carolina. A scheme that was conceived in iniquity and born in sin. And I am thankful tonight that I am permitted to have the privilege of raising my voice, though feeble, against wrong and oppression, and on behalf of right, liberty and justice. For "thrice is he armed who hath his quarrel just."

We are here tonight, Mr. President, asking on behalf of over one hundred thousand loyal, devoted, patriotic sons—yea, and more the common people, the mudsills and prosperity of this historic old state—that the sacred and vested right of the elective franchise be not wrested from them at a single blow. And we come only pleading for this right in all that is fair, humane and just.

We come not as mendicants or pariahs, but as loyal taxpaying citizens. Not as office hunters or disturbers of the peace, but as humble, patriotic Carolinians demanding justice. Not as anarchist or socialist, floating the red flag of defiance and war for the destruction of American institutions, but as an industrious and law-abiding people; vested with full political rights vouchsafed and guaranteed to us under the constitution of this grand and magnificent republic. And as freemen, as American citizens, as Carolinians to the manor born, we protest against this everlasting and eternal prescription of being perpetual aliens.

We are unwilling to be dispossessed of our common heritage—the right of the ballot. For taxation without participation and representation is undemocratic and un-American. Are we destined to be a race of miserable crouching slaves in the land of Washington, Franklin, Jefferson, Samuel Adams and Patrick Henry? Here, where it is said and claimed that the common law and free institutions give protection to the weak and hold back the encroachments of the strong and secure to every man the reward of his honest labor, as an inheritance to the generations that are yet to come.

For, Mr. President, it is one of America's cardinal doctrines published from the pulpit, proclaimed from the rostrum and inculcated in the common schools that political and commercial liberty, liberty of speech and the liberty of the press are the fundamental and underlying principles of any government and are essential to their prosperity and happiness.

Now, gentlemen, I have too much faith in the fairness and integrity of the Anglo Saxons of South Carolina. The descendant of an illustrious and noble ancestry, the scions of the Huguenot fathers and the landed gentry of old England, a people who represent the best and highest type of American and Christian civilization, to entertain the idea or believe at all that they would be so un-Christian, unchivalrous, unjust and dishonest as to so humiliate and degree one class of citizens, because forsooth, the hue of their skin and the texture of their hair are unlike their own.

Remember, we have no privileged class in our country, and the man who acknowledges one is unfit to be a freeman, for, "Honor and shame no condition rise. Act well on your part—there, all the honor lies." Is it not enough to awaken in every true loyal American heart a feeling of just indignation that after the wonderful progress, the remarkable growth and the great strides the Negro has made intellectually and financially in thirty years, for the civilized world today stands amazed and astonished to behold how a people so recently liberated from the iron heels of slavery have so prospered. Yea, even beyond the most hopeful and sanguine expectations of their friends, are now to be thus degraded and made political serfs by being denied the free exercise of the ballot. And for what cause?

We surely are endeavoring to attain a better and higher citizenship that we may secure the blessings which belong to us and to our own children. We

72

are aware that a good citizen is a standing safeguard and constant surety for the preservation of the peace and good order of the state and country. Then why this disfranchisement? Remember, gentlemen, that the history of the world repeats itself. Remember, "That Brutus was the fanatic of a faction; Caesar the true representative of the whole Roman people."

Mr. President, we are told the law of injustice will roll on and on and on until it reaches its climax, and then a reaction is bound to come, which has already been verified in the nefarious and damnable registration and eight box law, which you are now trying to prop up by a scheme even more diabolical. It is a living truism, "When you dig a pit for your brother, dig one for yourself also."

Where are the sponsors of that law that has forever rolled the escutcheon of South Carolina and has brought dishonor upon her fair name? Echo answers where? Where are the [Wade] *Hamptons,* [Johnson] *Hagoods,* [George] *Leapharts,* [Hugh] *Thompsons,* [William Gilmore] *Simms and* [Pierce] *Butlers, the representatives of an effete aristocracy who have been stigmatized as enemies of the common white people of South Carolina and driven from the hustings, yea, from place and power, regulated forever to the shades of political quietude?*

Now, the so-called understanding clause that is incorporated in the ordinance that is recommended by the committee is so hedged in and beset on every side that it shows on its face plans and give the white women the most palpable and glaring fraud. It is nothing but a political jack ketch. In a nutshell, it proposes to disenfranchise one class of citizens and enfranchise another, who in many cases are more illiterate, ignorant and unfit to exercise the rights of the elective franchise than the one it seeks to disenfranchise.

Senator Tillman said in a speech this summer, "That the right to judge the qualification of a voter rest with the supervisor of registration and that you must rely upon the administration rather than the language of the law." Then he goes further and says, "If the applicant can read, he must be registered and therefore entitled to vote." Now it appears that he doesn't mean what he says as to a white applicant's qualification to read or not, for in the next breath, he says, "It is easy to see that the Negroes could not understand where the white man would." The Negro would not understand the section when read to him because he is a Negro and because the man who will judge of his understanding is white.

Can words in the English language express more clearly that the intention of this plan is founded. You were told at the beginning of this convention, in an address delivered by one of the lady advocates of woman suffrage, to do away with your fraud-producing plans and give the white women of South Carolina the right to vote so that you may not commit a crime upon a patient and long-suffering people.

The Honorable George D. Tillman intimates that your plan was fraudulent when he told you a few days ago that he knew of no method of obtaining white supremacy in the state through fair and honest means, unless you adopt the township plan of government. Senator Irby says your plan is a political monstrosity. Now these are names piled high in the political firmament in our state and country, well versed in the art of political science and economy, and their opinions are worth much and are worthy of consideration.

But sirs, I suppose the passage of the committee recommendation is inevitable. The fiat has gone forth and like the laws of the Medes and Persians—irrevocable. Then let it come. But to quote the words of the editor of the Greenville News:

"Does it settle anything or remove the Negro from politics as we were promised it should? A thing to remember is that the full white vote will be registered at the beginning. After that, its increase must follow the natural increase or any that may come from immigration. On the other hand, every Negro who learns to read and write or who acquires $300 worth of property will be a new voter. A new stimulant is given to the ambition of an already ambitious race. The whites will start with their largest number of votes. The Negro starts with his smallest number and will climb steadily. How many years will he need to creep up and up, or how long will it be before he establishes alliances? Instead of being taken out of politics, the Negro is put in deeper than ever, and white supremacy is guaranteed only while there is white unity. We were precisely in that condition before."

But it appears, Mr. President, that zealots profit not by the teachings of history and have yet to learn that the blood of the martyrs is the seed of the church, and eminent writers have said that the fundamental principles of justice, of righteousness, of loyalty to the truth, of uncompromising opposition to all that is wrong must be implanted in the hearts of our people and must be brought to bear on all our civic life and dealing with each other.[30]

"By My God, By My Country"
Isaiah Reed's Message

Not long after Anderson's address, Isaiah R. Reed, a Beaufort lawyer, addressed the convention, according to the *Charleston News and Courier*'s October 29, 1895 edition.

Mr. President and gentlemen of this convention:

In the early days of the settlement of this great American country, two ideas diametrically opposed to each other were fostered and cherished in the mind and heart of the American people. I refer on the one hand to that precious boon of mankind known as liberty, the seeds of which were first sown within the confines now known as the commonwealth of the state of Massachusetts. On the other hand, I refer to that great drawback and abomination known as slavery, which was planted and nourished in incipiency within the area of the state or commonwealth of Virginia.

These two ideas, though foreign to each other, grew and flourished as a tree with American citizenship, and moved on and on with a parallel with each other westward across the country according to the trend of immigration and settlement. Liberty carried with it the right and privilege to grow and expand intellectually, socially, morally and politically, in short, everything that goes to make up a full-fledged citizen, while slavery curtailed and obstructed such rights and privileges. And of all the early American citizens and statesmen, no one had a keener sensitiveness and buoyancy and enlightening influence of the one and humiliating and degradation of the other than Patrick Henry, when from the power of the slavery made by the power of the mother country, he uttered those memorable and laconic words, "Give me liberty or give me death." This sentiment has been published throughout the American colonies and become their byword during the struggle for independence, and later in 1812. The part in which the Negroes played in these two struggles has already been admirably portrayed and vindicated by my colleagues who have preceded me, and I cannot enter the discussion of it unless I trespass upon their thoughts.

This love of liberty has grown in the hearts of the people of the United States of America until it bubbled and bloomed into the unmistakable and impressive sentiment and words of the preamble to the federal Constitution, namely, "We the people of the United States, in order to form a more perfect union, establish justice, insure domestic tranquility, provide for the common defense, promote the general welfare, and secure the blessings of liberty to ourselves and our posterity do ordain and establish this Constitution for the United States of America."

The articles which followed this masterpiece of literature need not herein be stated. But suffice it to say that the delegates from South Carolina, John Rutledge, the two Pinckneys [Charles and Charles Coatesworth Pinckney], *and Pierce Butler, signed the said Constitution, and after ratification, the State of South Carolina was made a party to this great, grand and glorious political contract, which has withstood the tests of judicial courts, the darts of public opinion and the tension of internal strife.*

This being done, liberty was sealed up in the nation's great political vault in such a manner that "he who runs may read." Still, the question may be asked, "Liberty to do what?" Well, among some things other than those stated above, it was liberty to have the accuser and accused face to face; liberty to be tried by a jury of their own countrymen; liberty to be taxed and pay taxes to their own established government; and liberty to vote for and be ruled by their own ruler.

While this was going on, slavery sat as a sceptered hermit in the republic; and it and liberty met and confronted each other for the first time on the soil of the state of Missouri, when Henry Clay, for the time being, by his famous Missouri Compromise, averted a conflict to be renewed in the great intestine war of 1861–65. Now the causes of that great struggle for supremacy need not herein be stated, but the result of it was that it did form a more perfect Union, it did establish justice, it did provide for the common defense, it did promote the general welfare and secured the blessings of liberty to all of the citizens and their prosperity when the Thirteenth, Fourteenth and Fifteenth amendments were accepted and made the Negroes full-fledged citizens of the United States and of the states. You have charged that the Negroes are ignorant and that they are prone to elect ignorant and unscrupulous men to office. Does not the intelligence of the delegates here from Beaufort refute that charge? You have suffered the Negroes to harness in tandem and drive your costly steeds through the thoroughfares; you have suffered them to serve the delicacies of your festal board; in short, you have suffered them to attend many other vocations of life, which come nearer to your person and nearer to your property than casting a ballot.

Can any delegate here deny that no Negro voted for him to be a delegate to this convention? Will anyone also deny that no Negro voted for [Wade] *Hampton, or* [former South Carolina governor Johnson B.] *Hagood, or* [former South Carolina governor John Calhoun]

Sheppard, or Hugh Thompson, or [former South Carolina governor John P.] *Richardson? I will go further; will one deny that since the reform movement was ushered into the politics of this state that the Negroes did not vote for the Honorable Benjamin R. Tillman, the chairman of the suffrage committee, or the present governor of this state, who is now president of this convention? And are not these facts sufficient to refute the charge that Negroes did not vote for what you would call good government, but desire to predominate? There has never been, or is there, any Negro domination threatened this.*

This convention and the suffrage plan thereof is brought about by the political strife between the one faction, which is called the conservative on the one hand, and the reformers on the other, and the delusion of "Negro domination" to solidify the whites in perfecting a suffrage scheme that would drive the Negroes to the political wall. But the ignorant white voters and the Fourteenth and Fifteenth Amendments to the federal Constitution stand in the way. And a little reflection on this political strife brings to mind the following story that runs thus: One bird said to another, "I have two eyes." The other said, "So have I." "I have two feet." "So have I." "I have two wings." "So have I." "What is the difference between you and me?" "Well, you flap your wings against the wooden gates of the barnyard, and I flap my wings against the golden gates of the sun." The conservatives have been flapping their wings against the political golden gates from Hampton to Richardson, while the reformers flapped their wings against the political wooden gates, but things are vice versa now, and on the adoption of this suffrage plan, some other party may flap its wings against the political golden gates.

Now, you members on the Democratic side declare that ignorance predominates in this state. Your patriotism, therefore, should be to provide a suffrage scheme that is favorable to the greatest number. But instead of that, you have proposed a political spider web to abridge the rights and immunities of the majority. Now, take the same class of citizens, the poor and ignorant whites and Negroes in the militia of the state. You suffer him to bear and put on the armor of the state and call upon him to stop insurrection and to keep the peace and dignity of the state, yet he is not permitted to vote for the officers whose duty it is to order him out to do so. Let us go further and see how this same class of citizens as he comes into the courts. He is brought before the trial justice who gives him all trials and no justice. He is sent to the upper courts and after the indictment is read to him, he is asked the question, "How will you be tried?" And he cannot conscientiously answer, "By my God and by my country," because it is not his since he cannot take part in voting for the men who make the laws under which he is charged and who are to decide his destiny.

In conclusion, I say that all such things produce bad and revolutionary citizens and stop the citizens from defending and honoring the peace and dignity of the state. That these citizens should be defended by a fair and impartial suffrage that would not commit them to the mercy of arrogant and unscrupulous registrars and managers who could invert, subvert, overt, divert their political wishes.

Whipper and Smalls proposed their own voting rights plan that involved the following provisions, which was ultimately defeated.

Section 1. In all elections by the people, the electors shall vote by ballot.

Section 2. Every male citizen of the United States of the age of twenty-one years and upwards, not laboring under the disabilities named in this constitution, without distinction of race, color or former condition, who shall be a resident of this state at the time of the adoption of this constitution, or who shall thereafter reside in this state one year, and in the county in which he offers to vote sixty days next preceding any election, shall be entitled to vote for all officers that are now or hereafter may be elected by the people, and upon all questions submitted to the electors at any elections; provided, that no person shall be allowed to vote or hold office who is now, or may be, disqualified therefor by the Constitution of the United States, until such disqualification shall be removed by the Congress of the United States; provided, further, that no person while kept in any alms house or asylum, or any of unsound mind, or confined in any public prison, shall be allowed to vote or hold office.

Section 3. It shall be the duty of the general assembly to provide from time to time for the registration of all electors.

Section 4. For the purpose of voting, no person shall be deemed to have lost his residence by reason of absence while employed in the service of the United States, nor while engaged upon the waters of this state, or the United States, or the high seas, nor while temporarily absent from the state, or removing from one house to another or from one place to another in the same precinct.

Section 5. No soldier, seaman or marine in the army or navy of the United States shall be deemed a resident of this state in consequence of having been stationed therein.

Section 6. Electors shall, in all cases, except treason, felony or breach of the peace, be privileged from arrest and civil process during attendance at elections and in going to and returning from the same.

Section 7. Every person entitled to vote at any election shall be eligible to any office, which now is, or hereafter shall be, elective by the people in the county where he shall have resided sixty days previous to such election, except as otherwise provided in this constitution or the Constitution and laws of the United States.

Section 8. The general assembly shall never pass any law that will deprive any of the citizens of this state of the right of suffrage, except for treason, murder, robbery or dueling, whereof the persons shall have been duly tried and convicted.

Section 9. Presidential electors shall be elected by the people.

Section 10. In all elections, state and federal, there shall be but one ballot box and one ticket for each party or faction thereof, with the names of all the candidates thereon. There shall be three commissioners of election for each county and three managers for each polling precinct, not more than two of whom shall be of the same political party.

Section 11. In all elections held by the people under this constitution, the person or persons who shall receive the highest number of votes shall be declared elected.

These measures were defeated after Reed's speech, according to the *Columbia State*'s October 29, 1895 edition. After all, the Black delegates voted in favor, and the white delegates voted against.[31]

"MY RACE NEEDS NO DEFENSE"
ROBERT SMALLS'S REPLY, NOVEMBER 1, 1895

On November 1, 1895, Benjamin Tillman, along with former South Carolina governor John Calhoun Sheppard, gave lengthy tirades against the alleged ignorance and criminality of the Black members of the South Carolina legislature, directing many of their remarks against Robert Smalls and William J. Whipper. At one point, as Sheppard accused Robert Smalls of being so guilty of fraud that it was admitted even by members of his own race. When Smalls rose amid this statement to defend himself, Sheppard rudely shouted, "You do not know what you are talking about! Keep your seat until I get through!" When Sheppard finished, Smalls said the following in his defense. This speech also contains a statement that bears the title sentence that appears on Smalls's monument next to his grave at the Tabernacle Baptist Church in Beaufort, South Carolina.

Mr. President: I had thought that I would not find it necessary to have a word to say in regard to this contest for the right of freemen, for the question had been ably presented by others; but to my surprise, I find the distinguished gentlemen from Edgefield, Mr. B. Tillman and Mr. J.C. Sheppard, going away from the all-important question, the right to let free Americans cast an honest ballot for honest men.

By those gentlemen, I am arraigned here and placed on trial for an act said to have been committed in 1873 in South Carolina. It is true, sir, that I was arrested in the state in 1877, charged by the Democrats of the state with receiving a bribe in 1873. This was done after the Democratic Party had taken charge of state affairs; but the evidence upon which this trumped-up charge was brought was that of one Josephus Woodruff, who was clerk of the Senate and also public printer of the state and who had acknowledged that he had robbed the state out of over $250,000 and had run away and was brought back from Pennsylvania by a writ issued on the governor of that state.

This man Woodruff testified that of twenty checks, which he had given to "cash" or to "bearer," one was given to Robert Smalls. Why so?

Simply because they found that I had deposited in the Banking and Trust Company of the State $5,000 on the eighteenth day of January 1873. But when they went to examine the record, they found that the check in question was drawn on the nineteenth day of said month. On examining the calendar, they found that the nineteenth day of January was Sunday *and that if the check was given to me on that day, I could not have deposited until the twentieth.*

The gentleman, Mr. Sheppard, a few moments ago, said that I was convicted, the testimony being corroborated by the cashier of the bank. That gentleman was a member of the committee; but, sir, he could not have read the record in this case. The cashier of that bank was a man named Jacobs, who had been charged, as the record shows, under four indictments for perjury, and had fled the state, and a man by the name of Zealy brought in a little slip of paper, written in pencil, and said it was the handwriting of Mr. Jacobs, the cashier of the bank. Mr. Woodruff himself testified that he had made arrangements to borrow money or had been trying to do so and asked me to loan him $85,000 and that when I brought the money to him, he had already made the arrangements to get $820,000 from Dr. Zeagly. I am as innocent of that charge as you are.

But, sir, that matter is brought in here. The State of South Carolina was in the hands of the Democratic Party. It has been said that Judge Townsend was a Republican. This is the first I have ever known of it. He was not elected as a Republican but as a Democrat from Marlboro County, and today stands here as a Democrat. No one ever heard of Judge Townsend in the Republican ranks anywhere or at any time until now it seems convenient to serve a Democratic purpose.

The gentleman said that I was convicted by a jury of colored men or Republicans. Mr. Speaker, there were two colored men that might have been Republicans on that jury; but every man on that jury had been a Democrat and had worked and voted for Wade Hampton. There is Joe Taylor. Where is he today? Somewhere in Canada. He is a good Democrat, but he stole twenty bales of cotton the other day and has now gone somewhere else. I stand here today and am just as innocent of the charge as either of the gentlemen from Edgefield, who have gone out of the way to make this personal onslaught.

Now, let me say that after that trial and after I was arrested, I appealed to the supreme court of the state. The supreme court held that opinion off over one year, as the record will show. After I had run for Congress a second time, the supreme court rendered a decision sustaining the action of the lower court. After that was done, under Section 9 of the Revised Statutes, I took an appeal to the Supreme Court of the United States. I went to Washington and appeared before that court. The record shows I went before Chief Justice Waite, and he granted the appeal and docketed the case.

No sooner was this done and no sooner had I returned to South Carolina than, without a single word from me or a friend of mine, directly or indirectly, Governor Simpson, of South Carolina, issued and sent to me in Beaufort a pardon which I have here in this paper.

Mr. President, my acts in defense of my name and honor are such as are entitled to the respect of every freeman. I did all that man could do; but without my knowledge, against my will, the attorney general of South Carolina Mr. Youmans went before the United States Supreme Court and asked that the case be stricken from the docket, on the ground that it had been adjudicated in the state. I knew nothing of this at all until I happened to see a sketch of it in the News and Courier, *published in Charleston, saying that Mr. Youmans was in Washington and had made such a motion.*

But while I was in Columbia, before the trial came off, Mr. Cochrane, the chairman of that great investigating committee appointed by the legislature of South Carolina, said to me, "Smalls, you had better resign." Resign what?" "Resign your seat in Congress." "What?" said I. "The seat the people elected me to serve?" "Yes; you had better resign, because if you don't, they are going to convict you." Said I: "I don't believe that. sir. I am innocent, and they cannot do it." "Well," said he, "bear in mind that these men have got the court, they have got the jury and an indictment is a conviction." I did not believe it, but I tell you those gentlemen taught me it was so. And it was so. I was sought by another gentleman, a gentleman from Aiken County, Mr. Drayton, the editor of a paper there. He came to me and said: "Smalls, we don't want to harm you. Get out of the way. We know you were kind to our people just after the surrender, and Governor Hampton says he doesn't want to injure you. We want this government, and we must have it. If you will vacate your office, we will pay you $10,000 for your two years' salary," said Mr. Drayton. "Where did you get this money to give me?" Said he, "Smalls, don't you ask that. We have got the money. The people of South Carolina have paid in 10 percent on their taxes to perpetuate the Hampton government, and we intend to have it." Said I: "Sir, if you want me to resign my position, you must call meetings all over the congressional district and get those people who elected me to pass resolutions requiring me to resign, and then you can have the office without a penny. Otherwise, I would suit myself to go into the penitentiary and rot before I would resign an office that I was elected to a trumped-up charge against me for the purpose of making me resign."

Make me resign when I am innocent; make me resign when the only testimony against me is that of a self-confessed thief. And, Mr. President, this self-confessed thief at my trial admitted, under oath, that he had been granted immunity from trial because he had promised the prosecution to testify against me. And, Mr. President, this man Woodruff has never been tried.

Why should this matter be dragged into this debate? Why, sir, it is to inflame the passions of delegates against Republicans and force them to vote for this most infamous Suffrage Bill, which seeks to take away the right to vote from two-thirds of the qualified voters of the state.

It has been claimed that there has been a compromise in my case, but this is not true. I refused all offers of compromise, but there were compromises made but I was not included; I received no advantage therefrom. I have here a copy of a compromise entered into by the State of South Carolina and the United States district attorney for South Carolina, which I send to the desk and ask that it be read, which speaks for itself:

Executive Department.
Office of the Attorney-General,
Columbia, SC, April 22, 1879.
Hon. L.C. Northup, U.S. District Attorney for the District of South Carolina,

Charleston, SC

Dear Sir: After seeing in writing the views of the governor and the state delegations in both branches of Congress, and after consultation with the state officers and others, I have deemed it proper, in the interests of peace and quiet in the state, to address you this letter in regard to the action thought to be the most conducive to that end and most practicable under the circumstances, as to certain prosecutions which have been, or may be, brought by the United States and state governments respectively.

That action is that the United States government shall continue the cases against all persons charged with violations of law by the commission of any acts whatever in connection with, or growing out of, past canvasses or elections, and at the next term, or as soon thereafter as practicable, not prosecute them, and that no more prosecutions shall be had.

That upon this continuance by the United States, the state shall continue the pending cases against D.H. Chamberlain and others, brought under the resolution of the general assembly, and all cases against persons charged with violations of law by the commission of any acts whatever in connection with, or growing out of, past canvasses or elections, and all cases of criminal malfeasance on the part of any public officers of the state, or of bribery or corruption of the public officers of the state, prior to January 1, 1877, and not prosecute the same, upon the United States not pressing the prosecutions aforesaid brought by the United States government, and that no more such prosecutions shall be had by the state.

If you will do what is necessary to carry this out, as United States attorney, I will do what is necessary to carry it out as attorney general.

Very respectfully,
[Signed] *LeEoy F. Youmaxs.*
Attorney General, South Carolina
Charleston, SC, April 29, 1879

I certify that the above is a true and exact copy of a letter handed to me today after the cases alluded to were continued in the United States Court.
[Signed] *L.C. Nokthbop*

True copy of the certified copy as above in L.C. Nokthbop's handwriting.
[Signed] *Warren E. Marshall*
April 30, 1879.

Mr. President, I am through with this matter. It should not have been brought in here. All the thieves are gone; they are scattered over the nation, but I have remained here. My race has honored me with a seat on this floor, and I shall serve them to the best of my ability. My race needs no special defense, for the past history of them in this country proves them to be the equal of any people anywhere. All they need is an equal chance in the battle of life. I am proud of them, and by their acts toward me, I know that they are not ashamed of me, for they have at all times honored me with their votes.

No matter what is said, I believe that the members [of the convention] *came here with so much determination to do away with the Negro vote that now they don't seem to stop at anything, but they found out that we are able to take care of our race, and they do not want us to show ourselves. God knows I am innocent of any charge of fraud. I never received a dollar fraudulently from the state. I stand here the equal of any man. I started out in the war with the Confederates; they threatened to punish me, and I left them. I went to the Union army. I fought in seven battles to make glorious and perpetuate the flag that some of you trampled under your feet.*

Innocent of every charge attempted to be made here today against me, no act or word of yours can in any way blur the record that I have made at home and abroad.

Mr. President, I am through, and shall not hereafter notice any personal remark. You have the facts in the case; by them, I ask to be judged.[32]

"THE NEGRO WILL RISE"
WILLIAM WHIPPER ANSWERS BENJAMIN TILLMAN

A major portion of Tillman's argument for this convention were the charges of corruption against the Reconstruction government in South Carolina, particularly those charges against Black officeholders, such as William J. Whipper of Beaufort County. Whipper said the following statement in regard to Tillman's charges on November 1, 1895. In these remarks, Whipper referred to Daniel Chamberlain and Franklin J. Moses, both of whom served as governors of South Carolina during the Reconstruction era. Near the end of his message, Whipper gave perhaps the most outspoken, if not the most eloquent, response to the convention.

I am reluctant to defend myself. I feel that I have lived long enough and far enough above such charges to notice them, but when they come as they did last night, I must answer. Chamberlain refused my commission on the grounds of incompetency, but Chamberlain was there, trying to be made the compromise candidate. The whites honey-fuggled around Chamberlain until they got him to send that message about the civilization of the Cavalier and the Puritan being in danger. As to my competency, I have nothing to say, and incompetency was the only charge against me. Chamberlain had afterwards said that if he could, he would give him one hundred judgeships, but that was when Chamberlain was a fugitive from justice, with the bloodhounds of the law after him. Chamberlain left the state, only to come back to dictate to it. I have been here all the time. I had never been away since 1866. As for the charges against me by Senator Tillman, no proofs were read against me.

At this point, Benjamin Tillman jumped up and shouted, "They are here! Will you deny that [Reconstruction governor Robert] Scott was not impeached and that he was not tried?" Whipper then replied:

I know, sir, and admit it that bribery had run riot through these halls. I announced that fact here long ago, and I regret that I only have part of my speeches here. I knew white men were bribed and did the bribing. No man has heard me defend that. I charge your papers with being subsidized. Long after that and at the time, there was no Democratic paper howling. You can tell the acts of the Negroes apart if you want to do so. I will never defend my race against what is known to be wrong. I now challenge you and Mr. Sheppard to point to any evidence that I was a bribe-taker. There is nothing in your record to show that. Get your letters and books and if you can show anything against me, I will send you my resignation to save you the trouble of expelling me. The only charge against me is that I received $3,000 for fitting up the hall of the House of Representatives. This was in the evidence of Dennis. If that were true, I would not show my face here or in the state.

I know there was no evidence of that charge outside the book of frauds. To be perfectly honest, I had no charges against the book. So far as I am concerned, I am willing to accept its statements. The committee reported the $3,000 matter, and I, immediately upon hearing of the report, communicated with the House of Representatives. I then advised the House that I never received any such check or money for any such purpose. I voted for the resolution declaring the expenses for fitting up the hall a waste of money and I was dismissed from the committee. With that record, I could not see how such a charge could even be seriously entertained. This is one of the two charges against me. If I could command $3,000 while off the committee, I could have secured more while on the committee. I am no fool, and a man who could have commanded a better price and was in the bribe-taking business would have known how to get the best price.

At that time, I demanded an investigation. I did accept fifty dollars a day as counsel in investigating the affairs of the bank. This was on account of the risk of not getting my pay, the value of the currency and the interference with my other professional work. I placed the committee at defiance. Woodruff and Dennis confessed their guilt and made up their statements accordingly. This was the first time I was ever called upon to defend myself in this way. I never expected to go over the matter again. I was secretary of the commission for about a year, I think.

Tillman then interjected, "Would you mind telling me about the Columbia and Greenville Railroad steal?" Whipper answered, "I was not on the board at that time." Tillman replied, "They had stolen it before you got on." Whipper then stated, "Then it saved my honesty." Tillman answered, "The point is that the radical legislature stole the money." Whipper then continued in his own defense:

> I was hooted down for calling attention to the steals that was going on. In 1872, I went into the Reform Republican Party. Then it was the paper in Charleston that was flopping for the young naïve governor. I was turned down for calling attention to the facts of the rottenness. Even my commission as brigadier general was snatched from me on account of my attitude. I could not charge ignorance against Mr. Patton and Mr. Tillman, and in their blind zeal to crush out, they have overstepped the bounds of—were I to say decency, it would be unparliamentary—but I would say a proper regard of the rights of the Negro delegates. Though we were humble in ability and numbers, yet we meant to conduct ourselves to deserve the respect of the word and this convention.
>
> This whole attack on the character of the Negro delegates is for the sake of working on public opinion. You, Mr. Patterson and Mr. Tillman, would besmear every Negro who went on the stand to defend his race. You use abuse instead of argument. This is done to say to the world that those Negroes talking there are all mixed up with those old frauds. It is to be an excuse for future generations. You want something that will deceive the world and yourselves. When you shall have passed your understanding clause, you can justify it if you will. Put it in there and you will call a convention in the next three years to remedy the error. The Negro is not disturbing you. He is your laborer, and for 200 years, he has been your laborer. Other states have marched on to prosperity, while you are trying to keep down the Negro and crush him out with the iron heel. For 240 years, slavery has held you back in chains, and the iron rust of those chains is still on the hearts of the people.
>
> This convention is about to make a great mistake in not giving the Negro latitude. The car of Negro progress is coming, and instead of allowing it to come on, you wish to stop it. You may just as well make up your minds that the Negro will rise. He will not be crushed. The Negro will rise, sooner or later, crush us as you may. The Negro, with his perseverance and pluck, will and must come out. He cannot be kept down forever. It is not the nature of human affairs.[33]

Even the *Charleston News and Courier*, which held little sympathy for the Black delegates, noted on November 2, 1895, "Mr. Whipper's statement in defense of himself and especially the closing part of his argument was generally conceded to be one of the finest speeches heard during the progress of the convention." As for Benjamin Tillman, he gamely moved that Whipper's remarks be placed in a journal of the convention, but this was about the only positive acknowledgement given to these two speeches by the convention.[34]

Representative William Henderson of Berkeley County gave the following reply to these speeches with words that flagrantly advocated a violation of the Fifteenth Amendment to the Constitution regarding the right to vote regardless of "race, color, or previous condition of servitude."

> *We don't propose to have any fair election. We will get left at that every time. Who will be the managers? Won't they be Democrats and Republicans, and don't you see that will be a bar to the Democrats? I tell you, gentlemen, if we have fair elections in Berkeley, we can't carry it. There's no use to talk about it. The Black man is learning to read faster than the white man. And if he comes up and can read, you have got to let him vote. Now are you going to throw it out? We are perfectly disgusted with hearing so much talk about fair elections. Talk all around, but make it fair, and you'll see what'll happen.*[35]

The *Columbia State*, on November 2, 1895, reported that laughter and applause greeted these latter remarks, and the *Charleston News and Courier* of that same date described Henderson as a "Berkeley Brave," who made "the star speech of the evening." The *Greenville Mountaineer* noted in remarks that were republished in the November 4, 1895 edition of the *Charleston News and Courier*, "The white majority in the convention listened with unexampled patience to the speeches of these Negroes, and we have no criticism to make that so much time was wasted."[36]

The six Black leaders who fought against the segregation convention in 1895. *Clockwise, starting at the top left*: Robert Anderson, Isaiah Reed, Robert Smalls, William J. Whipper, James Wigg, Thomas E. Miller. *From the Library of Congress, public domain*.

Clockwise, from top left: Senator Benjamin R. Tillman; George H. White; Robert Smalls as a young man; William J. Whipper. *From the Library of Congress, public domain.*

Clockwise from top left: Sarah V. Smalls, the daughter of Robert Smalls; Booker T. Washington; John R. Lynch, Congressman Oscar DePriest and Thomas E. Miller, 1931. *From the Library of Congress, public domain.*

3

BOOKER T. WASHINGTON'S PLEA TO BENJAMIN TILLMAN

Several weeks prior to the writing of the following letter, Booker T. Washington, the principal of the Tuskegee Institute in Alabama, became recognized as a major Black leader. Born into slavery in Virginia in 1856, he would walk some four hundred miles to the Hampton Institute to receive an education before helping found the Tuskegee Institute in 1881. His "Atlanta Exposition Address" endorsed a philosophy that encouraged diplomacy and friendly cooperation with white people in the face of segregation as a means of lessening racial problems. He felt this approach was necessary in the face of the opposition to any progress of Black Americans that was so great at the time. Washington was greatly criticized among some for this methodology, but he also secretly contributed to the protests against Jim Crow and occasionally spoke out on such matters, as evidenced by the following address. Washington's diplomacy caused the Tuskegee Institute to become one of the best-funded Black schools of that time, and in spite of criticism from many Black intellectuals, Washington became the most powerful Black man of his day.

Shortly after the Atlanta address, James Creelman of the *New York World* asked Washington to publicly comment on Benjamin Tillman's efforts to disfranchise Black residents in South Carolina, particularly in matters of education. This open letter to Senator Tillman appeared in the November 5, 1895 edition of the *New York World*.

Tuskegee, Alabama, November 4, 1895

Dear Sir:

I am no politician. I never made a political speech, and do not know as I ever shall make one, so it is not on a political subject that I address you.

I was born a slave; you a freeman. I am but one humble member of an unfortunate race; you are a member of the greatest legislative body on earth, and of the great, intelligent Caucasian race. The difference between us is great, yet I do not believe you will scorn the appeal I make to you on behalf of the sixty-five thousand of my race in your state, who are today suppliants at your feet and whose destiny you hold largely in your hands.

I have been told that you are brave, generous, and one too great to harm the weak and dependent; that you represent the chivalry of the South, which has claimed no higher praise than that of protector of the defenseless. I address you because I believe that you and those associated with you in convention have been misunderstood in the following, from the pen of Mr. James Creelman, in the New York World*: "An appalling fact that may not be obvious at a first glance is that the course proposed means the end of Negro education and Negro progress in South Carolina. This is openly admitted by Senator Tillman and his friends."*

It has been said that the truest test of civilization of a race is the desire to assist the unfortunate. Judged by this standard, the southern states as a whole have reason to be proud of what they have done in helping in the education of the Negro.

I cannot believe that on the eve of the twentieth century, when there is more enlightenment, more generosity, more progress, more self-sacrifice, more love for humanity than ever existed in any other stage of the world's history—when our memories are pregnant with the scenes that took place in Chattanooga and Missionary Ridge but a few days ago, where brave man who wore the blue and the gray clasped forgiving hands and pledged that henceforth the interests of one should be the interests of all—while the hearts of the whole South are centered upon the great city of Atlanta, where southern people are demonstrating to the world in a most practical way that it is the policy of the South to help and not hinder the Negro in the midst of all these evidences of good feeling among all races and all sections of our country, I cannot believe that you and your fellow members are engaged in constructing laws that will keep sixty-five thousand of my weak, dependent and unfortunate race in ignorance, poverty and crime.

You, honored senator, are a student of history. Has there ever been a race that was helped by ignorance? Has there ever been a race that was harmed by Christian intelligence? It is agreed by some that the Negro's schools should be practically closed because he cannot bear his proportion of the burden of taxation. Can an ignorant man produce taxable property faster than an intelligent man? Will capital and immigration be attracted to a state where three out of four are ignorant and where poverty and crime abound? Within a dozen years, the white people of South Carolina have helped in the education of hundreds of colored boys and girls at Claflin University and smaller schools. Have these educated men and women hindered the state or hurt its reputation? It warms my heart as I read the messages of the governors of Alabama, Georgia and other southern states, and note their broad and statesman-like appeals for the education of all the people, none being so Black or miserable as not to be reached by the beneficent hand of the state.

Honored sir, do not misunderstand me; I am not so selfish as to make this appeal to you in the interest of my race alone, for, thank God, a white man is as near to my heart as a Black man; but I appeal to you in the interest of humanity. The Negro can afford to be wronged; the white man cannot afford to wrong him. "Whatsoever a man soweth, that shall he also reap."

It is my belief that were it the purpose of your convention, as reported, to practically close Negro schoolhouses by limiting the support of these schools to the paltry tax that the Negro is able to pay out of his ignorance and poverty after but thirty years of freedom, his schoolhouses would not close. Let the world know it, and there would be such an inflowing of money from the pockets of the charitable from all sections of the country and other countries as would keep the light of the schoolhouse burning on every hill and in every valley in South Carolina. I believe, Senator Tillman, you are too great and magnanimous to permit this. I believe that the people of South Carolina prefer to have a large part in the education of their own citizens; prefer to have them educated to feel grateful to South Carolina for the larger part of their education rather than to outside parties wholly. This question I leave with you. The black yeomanry of your state will be educated. Shall South Carolina do it, or shall it be left to others?

Here in my humble home, in the heart of the South, I beg to say that I know something of the great burden the southern people are carrying and sympathize with them, and I feel that I know the southern people and am convinced that the best white people in South Carolina and the South are determined to help lift up the Negro.

In addressing you this simple message, I am actuated by no motive save a desire that your state in attempting to escape a burden shall not add one that will be tenfold more grievous and that we all shall act in the spirit of Him who when on Earth went about doing good that we shall have in every part of our beloved South a contented, intelligent and prosperous people.

Yours respectfully.[37]

Tillman did not reply to Washington, and the reduction in financing for Black education in South Carolina went on as planned. Washington's prediction of segregated education's harm to the overall education of South Carolina proved to be correct, as the literacy rates of South Carolinians hovered at low levels for the next century. By World War II, thousands Black and white South Carolinians were ruled too illiterate for military service, and in 1948, 62 percent of Black South Carolinians and 18 percent of White South Carolinians were reported to be functionally or totally illiterate, and South Carolina remained near the bottom of national rates in education.[38]

However, when Washington dined with President Theodore Roosevelt in 1901, Tillman responded, "The action of President Roosevelt in entertaining that nigger will necessitate our killing a thousand niggers in the South before they learn their place again." Interestingly, Washington would eventually meet Tillman and his wife while on a train ride from Washington, D.C., in 1909 and by Washington's own account, they had gotten along cordially. Tillman, for his part, would speak approvingly of his encounter with Washington, "Booker Washington is considered a great Negro, and he has great intellectual powers. He has a Jesuitical face."[39]

4

THE RESULTING VOTE

On December 4, 1895, the following articles were included in the South Carolina State Constitution regarding the right to vote in South Carolina.

Section 1. All elections by the people shall be by ballot, and elections shall never be held or the ballots counted in secret.

Section 2. Every qualified elector shall be eligible to any office to be voted for, unless disqualified by age as prescribed in this constitution. But no person shall hold two offices of honor or profit at the same time, except that any person holding another office may at the same time be an officer in the military and a notary public.

Section 3. Every male citizen of this state and of the United States twenty-one years of age and upwards, not laboring under the disabilities named in this constitution and possessing the qualification required by it, shall be an elector.

Section 4. The qualifications for suffrage shall be as follows:

(a) Residence in the state for two years, in the county one year, in the polling precinct in which the elector offers to vote four months and the payment six months before any election of any poll tax then due and payable; provided,

however, that ministers in charge of an organized church and teachers of public schools shall be entitled to vote after six months residence in the state, if otherwise qualified.

(b) Registration, which shall provide for the enrollment of every elector once in ten years and also an enrollment during each and every year of every elector not previously registered under the provisions on this article.

(c) Up to January 1, 1898, all male persons of voting age applying for registration who can read any section in this constitution submitted to them by the registration officer or understand and explain it when read to them by the registration officer shall be entitled to register and become electors. A separate record of all persons registered before January 1, 1898, sworn to by the registration officer shall be filed, one copy with the clerk of court and one in the office of the secretary of the state, on or before February 1, 1898, and such persons shall remain during life qualified electors unless disqualified by the other provisions of this article. The certificate of the clerk of court or secretary of state shall be sufficient evidence to establish the right of said citizens to any subsequent registration and the franchise under the limitations herein imposed.

(d) Any person who shall apply for registration after January 1, 1898, if otherwise qualified, shall be registered; provided that he can both read and write any section of this constitution submitted to him by the registration officer, or can show that he owns and has paid all taxes collectible during the previous year on property in this state assessed at $300 or more.

(e) Managers of elections shall require of every elector offering to vote at any election, before allowing him to vote, proof of the payment of all taxes, including poll tax, assessed against him and collectible during the previous year. The production of a certificate or of the receipt of the officer authorized to collect such taxes shall be conclusive proof of the payment thereof.

(f) The general assembly shall provide for issuing to each duly registered elector a certificate of registration and shall provide for the renewal of such certificate when lost, mutilated or destroyed, if the applicant is still a qualified elector under the provisions of this constitution, or if he has been registered as provided in subsection (c).

Section 5. Any person denied registration shall have the right to appeal to the court of common pleas or any judge thereof, and thence to the supreme court, to determine his right to vote under the limitations imposed in this article, and on such appeal the hearing shall be de novo and the general assembly shall provide by law for such appeal and for the correction of illegal and fraudulent registration, voting and all other crimes against the election laws.

Section 6. The following persons are disqualified from being registered or voting:

First. Persons convicted of burglary, arson, obtaining goods or money under false pretenses, perjury, forgery, robbery, bribery, adultery, bigamy, wife-beating, housebreaking, receiving stolen goods, breach of trust with fraudulent intent, fornication, sodomy, incest, assault with intent to ravish, miscegenation, larceny or crimes against the election laws; provided, that the pardon of the governor shall remove such disqualification.

Second. Persons who are idiots, insane, paupers supported at the public expense and persons confined in any public prison.

Section 7. For the purpose of voting, no person shall be deemed to have gained or lost a residence by reason of his presence or absence while employed in the service of the United States, nor while engaged in the navigation of the waters of this state, or the United States or of the high seas, nor while a student of any institution of learning.

Section 8. The general assembly shall provide by law for the registration of all qualified electors and shall prescribe the manner of holding elections and of ascertaining the results, of the same; provided, at the first registration under this constitution, and until the first of January 1898, the registration shall be conducted by a board of three discreet persons in each county, to be appointed by the governor, by and with the advice and consent of the senate. For the first registration to be provided for under this constitution, the registration books shall be kept open for at least six consecutive weeks, and thereafter, from time to time, at least one week in each month, up to thirty days next preceding the first election to be held under this constitution. The registration books shall be public records open to the inspection of any citizen at all times.

Section 9. The general assembly shall provide for the establishment of polling precincts in the several counties of the state and those now existing shall so continue until abolished or changed. Each elector shall be required to vote at his own precinct, but provisions shall be made for his transfer to another precinct upon his change of residence.

Section 10. The general assembly shall provide by law for the regulation of party primary elections and punishing fraud at the same.

Section 11. The registration books shall close at least thirty days before an election, during which time, transfers and registration shall not be legal; provided, persons who will become of age during that period shall be entitled to registration before the books are closed.

Section 12. Electors in municipal elections shall possess the qualifications and be subject to the disqualifications herein prescribed. The production of a certificate of registration from the registration officers of the county as an elector at a precinct included in the incorporated city or town in which the voter desires to vote is declared a condition prerequisite to his obtaining a certificate of registration for municipal elections, and in addition, he must have been a resident within the corporate limits at least four months before the election and have paid all taxes due and collectible for the preceding fiscal year. The general assembly shall provide for the registration of all voters before each election in municipalities; provided that nothing herein contained shall apply to any municipal election, which may be held prior to the general election of the year 1896.

Section 13. In authorizing a special election in any incorporated city or town in this state for the purpose of bonding the same, the general assembly shall prescribe as a condition precedent to the holding of said election a petition from a majority of the freeholders of said city or town as shown by its tax books, and at such elections, all electors of such city or town who are duly qualified for voting under Section 12 of this article, and who have paid all taxes, state, county municipal, for the previous year, shall be allowed to vote, and the vote of a majority of those voting in said elections shall be necessary to authorize the issue of said bonds.

Section 14. Electors shall in all cases except treason, felony or breach of peace, be privileged from arrest on the days of election during their attendance at the polls and going and returning therefrom.

Section 15. No power, civil or military, shall at any time interfere to prevent the free exercise of the right of suffrage in this state.[40]

It is important to consider that while this constitution does not openly say that citizens of African descent could not vote, it was filled with stipulations that amounted to that result to avoid an open challenge of violating the Fifteenth Amendment. Many Black workers in South Carolina were migratory in those days and thus were not likely to make the residency requirements of Section 4. Given the low salaries of Black South Carolinians at that time, it was unlikely that many would meet the requirement of $300 in property as stated in Section 4b or pay poll taxes as listed in Section 13. It is interesting that the crimes listed in Section 6 to disqualify voters did not include murder, as some members of the convention, such as the Tillman brothers, were members of violent organizations such as the Red Shirts who used force to stop Black voting in 1876. The crimes listed were those that were associated with Black miscreants. However, Section 4c was the most damaging to potential Black voters. It called for potential voters to be able to read a section of the state constitution to the satisfaction of present registrar. This allowed for illiterate white voters to be accepted while literate Black voters were mostly denied.

The final vote on the 1895 Constitutional Convention as 116 to 7. The Black delegates voted "no," with Whipper and Miller abstaining. Robert Smalls joined the other Black delegates in refusing to sign the completed constitution and declared that he would rather "walk home" to Beaufort before signing such a document. T.E. Dudley, a white delegate from Marlboro County, was one of the two white delegates who refused to vote for the 1895 Constitution. He expressed on the final day, "I voted 'no' on the final adaption of the constitution for the reason that there are many matters in the constitution that I voted against because I thought unwise and still hold to that opinion." John Harleston Reed, a white delegate from Georgetown, South Carolina, similarly stated, "My reason for voting 'no' on the question of adopting the constitution as a whole is: I have been from the beginning opposed to the understanding clause in the article on suffrage, believe it will be upset if tested in the United States [Supreme] Court, believe it opens the door for fraud and think it unnecessary, inasmuch as other provisions in the article, which are beyond suspicion of unfairness, will accomplish the desired end, i.e., securing white supremacy."[41] However, George C. Rogers speculated in his *History of Georgetown County, South Carolina* that Reed's vote was to "remain true to the forces that sent him to the convention"—in other words, the Black voters.[42]

The closing speech from George D. Tillman made no pretense of fairness to the state's Black population or the convention delegates of that race.

It must be a source of great gratification to every member here and to their constituents at home to see with what unanimity, with what courteousness and yet with what independence of action their representatives in this body have made the constitution which we have just ratified. It is a rainbow of hope that the state may hereafter be united, as in the past, as one man. For remember, my countrymen, it took all the efforts we could lay forth in '76, and for many years thereafter, to control this state; and if we become divided, as I fear we may be, and as I hope we will not for some time to come, we may find it still more difficult—I won't say impossible. I have an abiding faith in the Anglo-Saxon race, as there never has been a considerable number of them together anywhere that they did not dominate any race with which they came in contact; and whatever may happen, I have faith that they will rule. But as I said, let us never forget that it took the combined forces of all the men, women and children in South Carolina to get and keep control and that we ought to try in a spirit of self-sacrifice to come together here as we were in 1876.

Gentlemen, I will not detain you longer. I thank you for the high compliment you have paid me. Would to God I could have done more in my feeble way to help on the labors of this body. I have done my best, and so have you all. I hope that as South Carolinians, as white men and Democrats, we will go on as prosperously in the future as we ever have in the past. And no matter what shall betide us in the future, I believe we can meet any fate, and nothing can go amiss with us unless we forget that we are white men, Carolinians and Democrats.

After a long round of applause, it was with supreme irony that the white delegates gathered to sing "God Be with You till We Meet Again" before adjourning.[43]

As a result of the convention, Black voting was curtailed, schools were legally segregated and unequal and by 1898, public facilities began to be officially segregated in South Carolina. In 1896, the United States Supreme Court ruled seven to one in *Plessy v. Ferguson* that it was legal to segregate public facilities by race as long as equal facilities were provided. This law cemented the new dark ages that Black Americans would face in South Carolina and elsewhere until the modern civil rights movement. By 1899, North Carolina journalist Walter Hines Page observed the conditions of Black residents in Charleston under the new order and stated that he would rather "be an imp in Hades than a Negro in South Carolina."[44]

The speeches of Robert Smalls, Thomas Miller, William Whipper and their colleagues show that these developments did not take place without resistance.

5

THE RESPONSES

While most white southern newspapers responded with indifference to the plight of the Black delegates and the Black citizens they represented, a number of letters and telegrams were addressed to the Black delegates. Sarah V. Smalls collected them in her pamphlet of her father Robert Smalls's speeches at the convention.

The following is an editorial from the *New York Press*'s October 5, 1895 edition.

> *We can recall no more brilliant moral victory of a parliamentary minority than that gained on Thursday in the South Carolina Constitutional Convention by the representatives of the race about to be disfranchised for lack of intelligence wherewith to vote. In so characterizing the attack of these Black delegates, we have in mind the extraordinary ends accomplished with minorities by Mr. Randall, Mr. Blaine and Mr. Reed, the chief parliamentarians of our generation.*
>
> *In this case, the white majority laid themselves open to the flank movement, which Robert Smalls had evidently meditated throughout the session by introducing a quite superogatory article for the amendment of mixed marriages. The Black leader instantly moved an amendment providing that illicit as well as legal unions between the races should be prohibited. He proposed to disqualify all men—and this of course would mean only white men—who were parties to such unions. He proposed that the offspring of such unions should take their fathers' names.*

Senator Tillman, who seems, though the author of this new secession of South Carolina, to be the only man in the convention who appreciates in the slightest degree the effect of its actions upon outside public opinion, proceeded at once to save his record by espousing the Negro cause. He cut himself loose promptly from the majority in the course into which he knew its provincial ignorance would direct it. He went so far as roundly to berate his own chairman for his attempt to choke off the plea of the Black men for the integrity of Black women.

It was hardly a debate that followed. It was an arraignment which culminated when Mr. Smalls, after approving the punishment which lynch law has meted out to the worst offenders of his race, said: "If the same rule were applied on the other side and white men were treated likewise, I fear this convention would have to be adjourned for lack of a quorum."

The "burst of laughter" which followed this threw an interesting light on the morals and manners of South Carolina. It showed the state of civilization depicted in Tom Jones. *A convention composed entirely of squire westerns would have met such an impeachment in a precisely similar way. Having satisfied their sense of humor, the delegates killed the amendment and passed the mixed marriages article.*

This seizure of a parliamentary advantage in so sudden and effective a manner as to cause the majority leader to abandon his forces and leave them to expose their moral nakedness to the world was more than equal to Mr. Blaine's route of the Rebel brigadiers in the famous "Amnesty Debate." For those gentry managed to fan and sponge Ben Hill into the ring again, and these remained "out of time."

And in no one other way could the Negroes have so convincingly proved to the world their right to the ballot than by this victory of Black mind over white matter. It is now made plain, as it was made plain by the first laws passed by the un-Reconstructed legislature of the same state after the war, that the fear of Negro domination is not born so much of a regard for the numbers as for the developed intellectual ability of the Blacks. It is not Negro ignorance, but Negro intelligence, that is feared.

TELEGRAM.
Boston, MA, October 16, 1895. To the Honorable Robert Smalls, Columbia, SC:

Dear Sir: A body of clergymen and laymen in convention assembled in the city of Boston, Mass., congratulate you for the stand you took for virtue and chastity in the Constitutional Convention of South Carolina, on Oct. 2ᵈ, current. The Christian churches are with you in the struggle; indeed, the civilized world indorses the sentiment expressed by you. May God save the state of South Carolina from its barbarism.

[Signed] *Reverend W.M.H. SCOTT*
CLIFFORD H. PLUMMER, Sec
P.L. PEMBERTON

LETTERS OF CONGRATULATION
2121 North Twenty-Ninth Street
Philadelphia, October 30, 1895

Gen. Robert Smalls, Columbia, SC:

My Dear General—I am very desirous of procuring a copy of each one of the speeches delivered in your convention at Columbia on the suffrage question. If you have within easy reach any or all of them in print, I shall esteem it as a favor if you will kindly forward to me here such of them as you can readily spare. And let me say to you, my dear general, what has, I presume, been said to you already, that the dignity, courage and signal ability with which you and your Republican colleagues at Columbia, have asserted and maintained manhood rights and the just claims of all citizens to fair play under the supreme law of the land as well as under the civilization of our times, have touched the heart of the great North and called forth its soberest approval and its high admiration.

Indeed, it is felt here that, in your statements, your arguments and warnings, you have covered the whole case and done lasting honor to the Negro race and to American patriotism. All hail to you and your noble band of Spartans at Columbia!

Yours very sincerely,
E.C. BOSSETT

B.O. Duncan, a white delegate to the 1868 Constitutional Convention in Charleston, had this to say to Robert Smalls.

Newberry, October 28, 1895.
Honorable Robert Smalls:

Dear Sir: I take the liberty of expressing to you and through you to your colleagues, Messrs. Miller, Wigg and Whipper, my very great gratification and approval of your and their very able and eloquent addresses in behalf of sound Republican principles, of justice towards all classes, and of fair and honest elections. You all did credit to your race, to the Republican Party, and as I hope and believe to the cause of justice, for I have no doubt your efforts will have great influence outside the state. The prompt voting down of everything proposed, however fair and moderate, looked very much like preconcerted action and was not creditable to the convention, either conservatives or "reformers." But I should say, keep up the fight at every point along the line. Propos amendments to every objectionable section, even if they are voted down.

Very Respectfully,
B.O. DUNCAN.

A group of Black clergymen in Boston led by Reverend William H. Scott expressed their support for the Black delegates and their white supporters and added, "The Christian churches are with you in the struggle; indeed, the civilized world endorses the sentiment expressed by you. May God save the state of South Carolina from its barbarism." Horace Smith of London, England, compared these speeches to the writings of the great human rights fighter Frederick Douglass. However, one of the most heartfelt responses came from Robert Smalls's daughter Sarah V. Smalls, who stated in part in her pamphlet collection of the convention writings:

Indeed, it may have been an object lesson, planned by the all-wise God, to teach the haughty, boastful sons of Carolina that there are Negroes capable and amply qualified in every respect to protect themselves whenever it becomes necessary to do so; that those few representatives of the race were but a very small part of the rising host that time and education are bringing forward day by day in spite of lynching, caste prejudice or any methods used against them.[45]

The *Columbia State*, on November 27, 1895, reported that the Black community of Columbia gave a celebration to the Black delegates at the city's Odd Fellows Lodge Hall. The article noted that each of the six Black delegates attended and spoke at this occasion.[46]

In his biography on Robert Smalls, Andrew J. Billingsley commented:

> *They* [the Black delegates] *demonstrated a mastery of rhetoric and forensic skills as well as constitutional history, illustrating the important lesson that excellence in rhetoric, persuasion and deportment knows no race, creed or previous condition of servitude. It would be difficult to find a group of legislators today, Black or white, state or national, who could best these men.* [47]

But perhaps the most interesting commentary on the performance of the Black delegates survived in a folktale told in Orangeburg, South Carolina, in 1945 by a Black man named Murray Holiday to the South Carolina Negro Folklore Guild. A Negro spokesman at that convention was getting the best of Tillman in a debate. Tillman got angry and shouted, "You Black rascal, I've got a mind to swallow you alive." The Negro replied, "If you do, you'll have more brains in your belly than you do in your head!"[48]

6

CODA

As mentioned earlier, a few months after the constitutional convention, the Supreme Court ruled in *Plessy v. Ferguson* that laws segregating Black and white citizens in public places were constitutional. Several other southern states disfranchised Black voters in their state constitutions, among them Louisiana in 1898, and upon that occasion, the educator Booker T. Washington, like the Black South Carolina delegates, again raised his voice in response.

I beg of you, further, that in the degree that you close the ballot box against the ignorant, you open the schoolhouse. More than one-half of the people of your state are Negroes. No state can long prosper when a large percentage of its citizenship is in ignorance and poverty, and has no interest in government. I beg of you that you do not treat us as an alien people. We are not aliens. You know us; you know that we have cleared your forests, tilled your fields, nursed your children and protected your families. There is an attachment between us that few understand. While I do not presume to advise you, yet it is in my heart to say that if your convention would do something that would prevent, for all time, strained relations between the two races, and would permanently settle the matter of political relations in one state in the south, at least let the very best educational opportunities be provided for both races; and add to this the enactment of an election law that shall be incapable of unjust discrimination, at the same time providing that in proportion as the ignorant secure education, property and character, they will be given the right of citizenship. Any other course will take from one-half of your citizens' interest in the state, and hope and ambition to become intelligent producers and taxpayers to become useful and virtuous citizens. Any other course will tie the white citizens of Louisiana to a body of death.[49]

Washington noted that the leading newspapers of New Orleans endorsed his idea, but the Louisiana Constitutional Convention followed the path of the other southern states' conventions. Ironically, Washington's prediction in his last sentence came to pass, as New Orleans erupted into a destructive race riot in 1900, fifteen years before Washington's death in 1915.[50]

The extent of the despair Black Americans felt during this era was perhaps best expressed by Newberry, South Carolina native Bishop Henry McNeal Turner of the African Methodist Church in his *Voice of Missions* newspaper on March 16, 1897.

Let every Negro in this country with a spark of manhood in him supply his house with one, two or three guns or with a seven or a sixteen shooter, and we advise him to keep them loaded and ready for immediate use, and when his domicile is invaded by bloody lynchers or any mob by day or by night, Sabbath or weekday, turn loose your missiles of death and blow your fiendish invaders into a thousand giblets.

We have had it in our mind to say this for over seven years, but on account of our Episcopal status, we hesitated to express ourselves thus, fearing it would meet the disapproval of the House of Bishops. But their approval or disapproval has done nothing to stop the fiendish murderers who stalk abroad and are exterminating my race, so we have now said it, and hereafter, we shall speak it, preach it, tell it and write it. Again, we say: get guns, Negroes! Get guns, and may God give you good aim when you shoot.

Meanwhile, Benjamin Tillman continued his crusade against the Black vote. In 1898, he spoke before a white supremacy rally in Fayetteville, North Carolina. A few months earlier, a Black newspaper editor named Alexander Manly published an antilynching editorial in which he said in that white women occasionally voluntarily engaged in sexual relations with Black men. Tillman stirred the crowd by shouting, "Why didn't you kill the nigger editor who wrote that? Send him to South Carolina and let him publish any such offensive stuff, and he would be killed!" This was one of the factors that led to a deadly race riot in Wilmington a short time later. During that same month, another race riot occurred in Phoenix, South Carolina, after Black residents attempted to vote on the encouragement of a white political leader named Thomas Tolbert. In the riot, eight Black people were killed, and many others fled the area for fear of mobs. Ironically, Tillman disapproved the latter action, telling a crowd in nearby Greenwood, "If you want to uproot the snake [of Black voting], go and kill the Tolberts. But don't bother poor Negroes who had nothing to do with the Tolberts."[51]

Tillman was truer to form in the United States Senate on March 23, 1900, regarding his actions and the majority of his colleagues at the South Carolina Constitutional Convention.

> *Mr. President, I have not the facts and figures here, but I want the country to get the full view of the southern side of this question and the justification for anything we did. We were sorry we had the necessity forced upon us, but we could not help it, and as white men, we are not sorry for it, and we do not propose to apologize for anything we have done in connection with it. We took the government away from them in 1876. We did take it. If no other senator has come here previous to this time who would acknowledge it, more is the pity. We have had no fraud in our elections in South Carolina since 1884. There has been no organized Republican Party in the state.*
>
> *We did not disfranchise the Negroes until 1895. Then we had a constitutional convention convened which took the matter up calmly, deliberately and avowedly with the purpose of disfranchising as many of them as we could under the Fourteenth and Fifteenth Amendments. We adopted the educational qualification as the only means left to us, and the Negro is as contented and as prosperous and as well protected in South Carolina today as in any state of the Union south of the Potomac. He is not meddling with politics, for he found that the more he meddled with them the worse off he got. As to his "rights"—I will not discuss them now. We of the South have never recognized the right of the Negro to govern white men, and we never will. We have never believed him to be equal to the white man, and we will not submit to his gratifying his lust on our wives and daughters without lynching him. I would to God the last one of them was in Africa and that none of them had ever been brought to our shores. But I will not pursue the subject further.*[52]

It may strike the reader as bizarre that the United States Senate would tolerate such an open admission to the use of violence against American citizens to violate the Fifteenth Amendment in its halls, but two years earlier, a Supreme Court case titled *Williams v. Mississippi* ruled that disfranchisement schemes, such as those carried in Mississippi and South Carolina, were legal. These new constitutions did not openly state that Black Americans were denied their right to vote, although voting registrars were free to reject potential voters at their discretion. However, the predictable result was that by 1901, there was only one Black congressman remaining, George Henry White of North Carolina. He said these concluding words in his farewell speech on January 29, 1901.

Mr. Chairman, before concluding my remarks, I want to submit a brief recipe for the solution of the so-called American Negro problem. He asks no special favors but simply demands that he be given the same chance for existence, for earning a livelihood, for raising himself in the scales of manhood and womanhood that are accorded to kindred nationalities. Treat him as a man; go into his home and learn of his social conditions; learn of his cares, his troubles and his hopes for the future; gain his confidence; open the doors of industry to him; let the words Negro, colored *and* black *be stricken from all the organizations enumerated in the federation of labor. Help him to overcome his weaknesses, punish the crime-committing class by the courts of the land, measure the standard of the race by its best material, cease to mold prejudicial and unjust public sentiment against him, and, my word for it, he will learn to support, hold up the hands of and join in with that political party, that institution, whether secular or religious, in every community where he lives, which is destined to do the greatest good for the greatest number. Obliterate race hatred, party prejudice and help us to achieve nobler ends, greater results and become satisfactory citizens to our brother in white.*

This, Mr. Chairman, is perhaps the Negroes' temporary farewell to the American Congress; but let me say, phoenix-like, he will rise up someday and come again. These parting words are on behalf of an outraged, heartbroken, bruised and bleeding but God-fearing people, faithful, industrious, loyal people—rising people full of potential force.

Mr. Chairman, in the trial of Lord Bacon, when the court disturbed the counsel for the defendant, Sir Walter Raleigh raised himself up to his full height and, addressing the court, said, "Sir, I am pleading for the life of a human being."

The only apology that I have to make for the earnestness with which I have spoken is that I am pleading for the life, the liberty, the future happiness and manhood suffrage for one-eighth of the entire population of the United States.[53]

Benjamin Tillman died from a cerebral hemorrhage in 1918. Alexander Manly, the Black newspaper editor who, in 1898, escaped a mob in Wilmington, North Carolina, that was encouraged in part by Tillman to lynch him after Manly's antilynching newspaper articles, was living in exile in Philadelphia at the time of Tillman's death. He perhaps spoke for many Black Americans when he was quoted as saying of Tillman, "I wonder who is making hash out of him in hell tonight?"[54]

By coincidence, George White also died in 1918, and ten years later, his prediction proved to be correct when Oscar De Priest of Chicago was the first Black American elected to Congress since 1901. On February 10, 1930, he brought along two special guests to Congress who were in town to speak at a Negro History Week celebration later that night. In the middle of that afternoon, De Priest rose and asked Speaker of the House Nicholas Longworth of Ohio for consent to speak to the House of Representatives for two minutes. Speaker Longworth asked if there was any objection from the House, and none was given.

De Priest proceeded to make the following speech.

> *Mr. Speaker and members of the House, I wish to call your attention to the fact that we have two ex-members of this House present today, and I wish to present them to you. One is ex-Congressman John R. Lynch, who served from the fifth district of Mississippi in the Forty-Third, Forty-Fourth, And Forty-Seventh Congresses. The other one is Thomas E. Miller, who served from the seventh district of South Carolina in the Fifty-First Congress.*

The all-white House of Representatives applauded after each man was introduced. De Priest concluded, "I am glad to have the privilege of presenting these gentlemen to you. They happen to be gentlemen of the racial group with which I am identified, so I am not the only one left."[55]

Seventeen years later, on July 12, 1947, in *Elmore v. Rice*, Charleston native and federal Judge J. Waites Waring struck down the restrictions for Black voters in South Carolina on a behalf of a Black plaintiff from Columbia named George Elmore against election official Clay Rice. When making his decision, Judge Waring stated, "It is time for South Carolina to rejoin the Union. It is time for South Carolina to fall in line with the other states and adopt the American way of conducting elections."[56]

THE LEGACY

The resistance of the Black members to the Constitutional Convention of 1895 was largely forgotten in South Carolina's history.

As many southern states proceeded to write history books for use in their public schools, they followed the pattern set by the United Daughters of the Confederacy. By the early 1900s, southern history textbooks were made to abide by a policy that glorified the Confederacy as a "lost cause," portrayed slavery as a benevolent institution and downplayed such aspects as lynching. In South Carolina, the standard history textbook for eighth graders from 1917 until the 1980s was Mary Simms Oliphant's *The History of South Carolina*. This was how the volume described the Constitutional Convention of 1895:

> *Constitution of 1895. The legislature, in the session of 1894, called for an election of delegates to form a constitutional convention. The election was held, and the convention met in Columbia in September 1895. There were reforms needed in many directions, but the first object of the convention was to redraft the election laws so as to give the white people protection against an overwhelming but illiterate Negro majority. The convention opened, committees were appointed and a constitution framed. The last constitution, the one of 1868, had been the work chiefly of aliens and Negroes without character. The constitution framed in 1895 is the one under which we live today.*

Later South Carolina history books that were written from a more objective point of view mentioned these events at the convention in some small detail. George Tindal's *South Carolina Negroes, 1877–1901* describes the subject across several pages and provides brief quotes from the delegates. Ernest Lander Hago's *A History of South Carolina, 1865–1960* mentions the role of the Black representatives of the 1895 Convention in passing, and I.A. Newby's *Black Carolinians: A History of Blacks in South Carolina from 1895 to 1968* briefly speaks of the Black delegates' response but discusses the results of the constitution in greater detail. Andrew Billingsley's biography of Robert Smalls, *Yearning to Breathe Free*, dedicates a chapter to the Black delegates' role in the 1895 Convention and is perhaps the most detailed public accounting of this event to date. But with the exception of the Billingsley book, which is layman-friendly and easily found in bookstores, these latter volumes were better known to the occasional college-level scholar of South Carolina history—not to the average South Carolinian. It is safe to say that the story of the Black delegates has been largely regulated to obscurity.

Robert Smalls was perhaps the best known of the six delegates. He was perhaps more famous for smuggling his family out of slavery aboard the Confederate ship *The Planter* in 1862. He served as a congressman during Reconstruction and a collector of the Port of Beaufort, South Carolina, until 1913, two years before his death. A school and street were named after him in Beaufort, and near his gravesite at Beaufort's Tabernacle Baptist Church is a monument of Smalls engraved with his words from the convention: "My race needs no special defense, for the past history of them in this country proves them to be the equal of any people anywhere. All they need is an equal chance in the battle of life."[57]

Thomas Miller went on to serve as the first president of South Carolina State College in Orangeburg, where the library bears his name. He was removed from his position by Governor Coleman Blease in 1911, after he opposed the segregationist governor's election. After Oscar De Priest invited him to appear before Congress, he died in Charleston in 1938.[58]

William J. Whipper, who was born in Pennsylvania in 1834, had an illustrious career. Along with Robert Smalls, he was one of two of the six delegates who spoke at both the 1868 and 1895 Constitutional Conventions of South Carolina. Along with Macon B. Allen and Robert Browne Elliot, Whipper was part of the first Black law firm in America, starting the practice in 1868 at 91 Broad Street in Charleston, South Carolina. After the 1895 Convention, he returned to Beaufort, where he died in 1907.[59]

Robert B. Anderson, according to a local history of Black people in Georgetown, South Carolina, taught school and was a postmaster in Georgetown, South Carolina. One website stated that he died in 1901, but no other source confirms this date or that of his birth. James Wigg's political involvement prior to the convention is covered in passing in the *South Carolina Encyclopedia* in an entry from Beaufort historian Lawrence S. Rowland, which concludes, "Wigg disappeared from the public record, and his date of death is not known." When the author of this book spoke with Dr. Rowland while visiting Beaufort in February 2020, he said that the latter was also true of Isaiah Reed.[60]

On December 27, 2020, the author of this book spoke with Marilyn Hemingway, a descendant of delegate Robert B. Anderson and a founding CEO of the Gullah Geechee Chamber of Commerce Lowcountry Business Organization, in her home in Georgetown, South Carolina, about her ancestor and the role he played in the 1895 Constitutional Convention. "Robert B. Anderson was married to my grandmother's cousin Chloe Dunmore, whose family helped build Bethel African Methodist Church here in Georgetown, in whose graveyard she was buried. I was told that he was involved in state politics, was well respected in Georgetown, and one of my aunts knew one of his sons."

This author proceeded to read from Anderson's speech before the convention that appears in this text. Hemingway appeared visibly moved and responded as follows:

> *It makes me very proud, and as you were reading this, it reminds me of our family history of civic involvement in Georgetown and Horry County. Maybe it's just in our DNA to be community advocates. It's exciting to realize that possibility.*
>
> *It's tragic that society has hidden this from us, because imagine the reaction of children learning that a local hero stood up to Tillman? It would give them the courage to stand up to what they face today.*[61]

NOTES

Chapter 1

1. *State Convention of the Colored People of South Carolina*, 23–26.
2. Bennett, *Before the Mayflower*, 482.
3. Oliphant, *History of South Carolina*, 313–16. For a look at the sociological impacts of the Oliphant book on race relations, as its various editions were used in South Carolina's classrooms until 1984 (including the author's eighth-grade South Carolina history class in 1978), see Will Moredock's "Corruption of the Innocent," which was published in the *Charleston City Paper* on May 9, 2012 (2).
4. Tindal, *South Carolina Negroes*, 10.
5. *Proceedings of the Constitutional Convention*, 354.
6. Miscellaneous Documents of the House of Representatives for the Second Session of the 46th Congress, 1879–80, vol. 5, no. 40, part 1, 517–18. J.B. Maxwell (around 1854–1940) was the author's maternal great-grandfather, and some of his background information comes from family oral histories. Sherryl Washington James, a librarian and the author's cousin, found this document.
7. "The Law and The Primary," *Charleston News and Courier*, August 29, 1892, 8.

Chapter 2

8. Fordham, *Voices*, 71–72.

9. "Dissatisfied Negroes," *Charleston News and Courier*, September 21, 1893, 5.

10. Article from the now lost *Charleston Enquirer*, reprinted in the *Charleston News and Courier*, April 26, 1895, 5.

11. "Chronicles of Zerrachaboam," *Columbia State*, August 26, 1892, 5, and May 16, 1895, 5.

12. "An Appeal to Uncle Sam," *Columbia State*, July 11, 1895, 1.

13. "Forgotten No More," *Charleston Post and Courier*, November 22, 2020, F1, F5.

14. *Journal of the Constitutional Convention*, 26–29.

15. Ibid., 123.

16. Smalls, *Speeches at the Constitutional Convention*, 16–19.

17. Ibid., 19; "All Niggers, More or Less," *Charleston News and Courier*, October 17, 1895, 6.

18. "All Niggers, More or Less," 6.

19. Fordham, *Voices*, 74.

20. "Now on the Suffrage," *Columbia State*, October 26, 1895, 1.

21. Ibid., 2.

22. "A 'Divorce' Measure," *Columbia State*, November 1, 1895, 1.

23. "Suffrage Settled," *Columbia State*, November 2, 1895, 1.

24. Miller, *Suffrage*, 2.

25. Lawrence S. Rowland, "Wigg, James," South Carolina Encyclopedia, https://www.scencyclopedia.org/sce/entries/wigg-james/.

26. "Speech of James Wigg," *Charleston News and Courier*, October 27, 1895, 2.

27. "Smalls and Whipper," *Columbia State*, October 27, 1895, 1–2.

28. Smalls, *Speeches at the Constitutional Convention*, 5–11.

29. Tindal, *South Carolina Negroes*, 61. For more on Anderson, see local historian Steve Williams's *Ebony Effects* (342). Williams is a member of Anderson's church, Bethel African Methodist Episcopal Church, in Georgetown.

30. "Another Black Man's Plea," *Columbia State*, October 29, 1895, 1.

31. "The Night Session," *Charleston News and Courier*, October 29, 1895, 2.

32. "Suffrage Settled," *Columbia State*, November 2, 1895, 1–2. This source also contains former South Carolina governor John Calhoun Sheppard's retort to Robert Smalls.

33. Ibid., 2.

34. "The Deed Is Done," *Charleston News and Courier*, November 2, 1895, 2.

35. Miller, *Suffrage*, 2.
36. Ibid., 5; "Suffrage Settled," *Columbia State*, November 2, 1895, 2; *Charleston News and Courier*, November 2, 1985, 2.

Chapter 3

37. Washington, *Autobiography*, 159–63.
38. Amy Donelly, "Literacy in South Carolina," South Carolina Encyclopedia, https://www.scencyclopedia.org/sce/entries/literacy/.
39. For Tillman's initial response to Washington, see Kantrowitz, *Ben Tillman*, 259. Washington's comments on his encounter with Tillman appear in Hardin, *Booker T. Washington*, vol. 10, 110. Tillman's version of this meeting was printed in the *Charleston Evening Post*, April 20, 1909, 1.

Chapter 4

40. Smalls, *Speeches at the Constitutional Convention*, 11–16.
41. *Journal of the Constitutional Convention*, 727.
42. Rogers, *History of Georgetown County*, 481.
43. *Journal of the Constitutional Convention*, 734.
44. Edgar, *South Carolina*, 450.

Chapter 5

45. Smalls, *Speeches at the Constitutional Convention*, 3, 20–26.
46. "The Six Banqeted," *Columbia State*, November 27, 1895, 8.
47. Billingsley, *Yearning to Breathe Free*, 179.
48. Spalding, *Encyclopedia*, 94.

Chapter 6

49. Washington, *Autobiography*, 218–19.
50. For details on the New Orleans Race Riot, see Ida B. Wells's pamphlet *Mob Rule in New Orleans*, which appears in Bay, *Ida B. Wells*, 339–94.
51. Zucchino, *Wilmington's Lie*, 125; Kantrowitz, *Ben Tillman*, 257–58.

52. Congressional Record, 56ᵗʰ Congress, first session, 3,223–224.
53. Justesen, *In His Words*, 205–6.
54. Zucchino, *Wilmington's Lie*, 351.
55. Congressional Record, 71ˢᵗ Congress, second session, 3,382.
56. "Right of Negroes to Vote in Primary Upheld by Waring's Decision," *Charleston Evening Post*, July 12, 1947, 1.

Chapter 7

57. Oliphant, *History of South Carolina*, 352. The inscription on Robert Smalls's gravestone was observed by this book's author during a visit to the Tabernacle Baptist Church in Beaufort, South Carolina, in February 2020.
58. Foner and Branham, *Lift Every Voice*, 807.
59. Lawrence S. Rowland, "Whipper, William J.," South Carolina Encyclopedia, https://www.scencyclopedia.org/sce/entries/whipper-william-j/.
60. Williams, *Ebony Effects*, 342; Conversation between the author and Lawrence S. Rowland at the St. Helena's Branch of the Beaufort County Library, February 2020.
61. Author's interview with Marilyn Hemingway, Georgetown, SC, December 27, 2020.

BIBLIOGRAPHY

Books

Bay, Mia, ed. *Ida B. Wells: The Light of Truth, Writings of an Anti-Lynching Crusader*. New York: Penguin Classics, 2014.

Bennett, Lerone. *Before the Mayflower: A History of Black Americans*. New York: Penguin Books, 1993.

Billingsley, Andrew. *Yearning to Breathe Free: Robert Smalls of South Carolina and His Families*. Columbia: University of South Carolina Press, 2007.

Edgar, Walter. *South Carolina: A History*. Columbia: University of South Carolina Press, 1998.

———. *The South Carolina Encyclopedia*. Columbia: University of South Carolina Press, 2006.

Foner, Philip S., and Robert James Branham, eds. *Lift Every Voice: African American Oratory, 1787–1901*. Tuscaloosa: University of Alabama Press, 1998.

Fordham, Damon L. *Voices of Black South Carolina, Legend and Legacy*. Charleston, SC: The History Press, 2009.

Hardin, Lewis, ed. *Booker T. Washington Papers*. Champaign: University of Illinois Press, 1972.

Justesen, Benjamin R., ed. *In His Words: The Writings, Speeches, and Letters of George Henry White*. Lincoln, NE: Universe Inc., 2004.

Kantrowitz, Stephen. *Ben Tillman and the Reconstruction of White Supremacy*. Chapel Hill: University of North Carolina Press, 2000.

Ladner, Ernest. *A History of South Carolina, 1865–1960*. Columbia: University of South Carolina Press, 1960.

Melick, Charles Wesley. *Some Thoughts on the Negro Question*. Washington, D.C.: D.H. Deloe, 1908.

Miller, Mary J., ed. *The Suffrage; Speeches by Negroes in the Constitutional Convention: The Part Taken by Colored Orators in Their Fight for a Fair and Impartial Ballot*. N.d.: Privately printed, 1896.

Newby, I.A. *Black Carolinians: A History of Blacks in South Carolina from 1895 to 1968*. Columbia: University of South Carolina Press, 1968.

Oliphant, Mary Simms. *The History of South Carolina*. Columbia, SC: The State, 1917.

Rogers, George C. *History of Georgetown County, South Carolina*. Columbia: University of South Carolina Press, 1970.

Smalls, Sarah V., ed. *Speeches at the Constitutional Convention by Gen. Robert Smalls with the Right of Suffrage Passed by the Constitutional Convention*. Charleston, SC: Enquirer Print, 1896.

Spalding, Henry D., ed. *Encyclopedia of Black Folklore and Humor*. Middle Village, NY: Jonathan David Publishers, 1971.

State Convention of the Colored People of South Carolina, Proceedings of the Colored People's Convention of the State of South Carolina, Held in Zion Church, Charleston, November 1865. Charleston: South Carolina Leader Office, 1865,

Tindal, George. *South Carolina Negroes, 1877–1901*. Columbia: University of South Carolina Press, 1952.

Washington, Booker T. *Autobiography: The Story of My Life and Work*. Atlanta, GA: J. L. Nichols and Company, 1901.

Williams, Steve. *Ebony Effects: 150 Unknown Facts about Blacks in Georgetown SC (With Complete Proof)*. Conway, SC: Waccamaw Press, 2012.

Zucchino, David. *Wilmington's Lie: The Murderous Coup of 1898 and the Rise of White Supremacy*. New York: Atlantic Monthly Press, 2012.

Government Documents

Congressional Record, Seventy-First Congress, second session.

Journal of the Constitutional Convention of the State of South Carolina. Columbia, SC: C.A. Calvo Jr., state printer, 1895.

Miscellaneous Documents of the House of Representatives for the Second Session of the 46th Congress, 1879–80, volume 5, number 40, part one.

Proceedings of the Constitutional Convention of South Carolina, 1868. New York: Arno Press, 1969.

Interviews

Author's conversation with Lawrence Rowland, PhD. St. Helena Library, St. Helena Island, SC. February 2020.

Author's interview with Marilyn Hemingway. Georgetown, SC. December 27, 2020.

Newspapers and Periodicals

Charleston Evening Post
Charleston News and Courier
Columbia State

INDEX

ABOUT THE AUTHOR

 amon L. Fordham was born in Spartanburg, South Carolina, and raised in Mount Pleasant, South Carolina, near Charleston. A graduate of the University of South Carolina and the College of Charleston, Fordham is the author of four books, including *True Stories of Black South Carolina* and *Voices of Black South Carolina* from Arcadia and The History Press. He is also a public lecturer and an adjunct professor of history at the Citadel and Charleston Southern University.

Visit us at
www.historypress.com